DIRTY DOZEN

One Dozen Powerful Marketing Methods That Can Make You Super Rich!

By **T.J. Rohleder**
(a.k.a "The Blue Jeans Millionaire")

BE SURE TO CHECK OUT OTHER GREAT TITLES FROM
THE BLUE JEANS MILLIONAIRE LIBRARY:

The Magic Pill
Total Success
The 2-Step Marketing Secret Than Never Fails!
The Wow Factor!
3 Steps to Instant Profits!
Instant Cash Flow!
Money Machine
The Power of Hype!
Stealth Marketing
Jump... And the Net Will Appear!
Think Bigger

TABLE OF CONTENTS

Introduction:

By T.J. Rohleder

YOUR FORTUNE IS WAITING

The above headline is amazing, but true!

It may sound like hype, but all the money you'll ever want and need is waiting for you!

Where is this money?

That's simple... It's in the wallets, purses, bank accounts, and available lines of credit that tens of millions of people are using on their credit cards right now.

These tens of millions of people are already spending this money like there's no tomorrow... They might as well be spending it with you!

Yes, there are tens of millions of people in America alone who are spending huge sums of their disposable income on a wide variety of products and services. All you have to do is get a very small percentage of them to spend their disposable income with you — instead of someone else — and you can make a fortune!

This book will show you how!

This book gives you 12 little-known marketing secrets that were first introduced though a weekly conference call that we do to help our clients become better marketers. And just like the sub-title of this book suggests, becoming a better marketer and mastering these ONE DOZEN powerful marketing methods can make you huge sums of money!

How much money?

Well, that's the SHOCKING part!

You see, when my wife, Eileen, and I decided to dedicate ourselves to learning all we could about Direct Response Marketing and to master every aspect of it to the best of our ability, we quickly brought in a total of...

Over $10-Million Dollars In Our First 5 Years!

Suddenly, we were rich! In fact, we had <u>more money</u> than we knew how to intelligently spend. But the most important thing was the fact that we had begun to master every aspect of marketing. And because of that, in our first 19 years alone, we generated a total of...

Over $114,000,000.00!

Yes, we started our Direct Response Marketing Company in the fall of 1988 with less than $300.00. And in our first 19 years, we brought in a total of over $114-Million Dollars!

So, when I tell you that the huge fortune you seek is out there waiting for you <u>RIGHT NOW</u>...

I Know What I'm Talking About!

All you have to do is use our powerful marketing ideas to offer people something they really want... Do this right, and millions of dollars can come pouring into your bank account!

Can it really be that simple?

Yes, it is! It's simple, but not always easy. In fact, the more money you want to make, the harder it can be. That's part of the challenge and should not discourage you.

And that brings me to the golden secret to your huge fortune!

Remember, all the money you want is waiting for you right now. I gave you part of the secret — which is creating products and services that people want the most. The other part of the secret to getting all of the wealth you seek is to...

Become a great marketer!

The more money you want to make, the more you must understand about marketing.

If you ask 1,000 different business experts what marketing is, you'll get some very complicated and confusing answers... But marketing is actually very simple. Here's my definition: Marketing is simply all of the things you do to get people to buy and re-buy from you as often as possible, for the largest amount of profit with each transaction. That's it! **When you learn how to do this the right way, you can bring in many millions of dollars — just like we have!**

Does that sound hard to believe? Well, it's true!

You see, the formula for wealth is so simple a junior high school student can understand it:

All you have to do is get enough people to continue giving you a large enough sum of money, for enough profit from each transaction, and you will ultimately make many millions of dollars!

Hang that quote on your refrigerator or bathroom mirror!

Then think about this:

The better you become at marketing, the more money you will make!

Marketing is the process you go through to attract and retain the very best customers who want what you sell. Just get enough people to consistently give you enough money... often enough... for a large enough profit margin per transaction and all the money you want will be yours. Yes, it's that simple! And when you COMBINE that idea with the 'DIRTY DOZEN' marketing secrets you'll get in this book, you can make all the money you've ever dreamed of making!

So please keep those simple ideas in mind as you go through this book. Have fun reading each chapter and THINK DEEPLY about how you can use all of the powerful ideas and strategies I'm about to share with you...

And to reward you for purchasing this book, I have...

A great FREE business-building gift for you!

Yes, I have a gift waiting for you that can
DRAMATICALLY INCREASE YOUR SALES AND
PROFITS! Here's what it's all about: I spent TEN FULL
YEARS writing down all of the greatest marketing and success
secrets I discovered during that time period. Each day, I took a
few notes and, at the end of a decade, I had a GIANT LIST of
6,159 powerful secrets! This list is ALMOST 1,000 PAGES of
hardcore money-making ideas and strategies!** **Best of all, this
massive collection is now YOURS ABSOLUTELY FREE!**
Just go to: www.6159FreeSecrets.com and get it NOW! As
you'll see, this complete collection of 6,159 of my greatest
marketing and success secrets, far more valuable than those you
can buy from others for $495 to $997, is absolutely **FREE.** No
cost, no obligation.

Why am I giving away this GIANT COLLECTION of
secrets that took ONE DECADE to discover and compile—
FOR FREE? That's simple: I believe many of the people who
receive these 6,159 secrets in this huge 955 page PDF document
will want to obtain some of our other books and audio programs
and participate in our special COACHING PROGRAMS.
However, you are NOT obligated to buy anything—now or ever.

I know you're serious about making more money or you
wouldn't be reading this. So go to: www.6159FreeSecrets.com
and get this complete collection of 6,159 of my greatest
marketing and success secrets right now! **You'll get this
GREAT FREE GIFT in the next few minutes, just for letting
me add you to my Client mailing list,** and I'll stay in CLOSE

TOUCH with you... and do all I can to help you make even more money with my proven marketing strategies and methods.

So with all this said, let's begin...

** WARNING: This complete collection of 6,159 marketing and success secrets contains MANY CONTROVERSIAL ideas and methods. Also, it was originally written for MY EYES ONLY and for a few VERY CLOSE FRIENDS. Therefore, the language is X-RATED in some places [I got VERY EXCITED when I wrote many of these ideas and used VERY FOUL LANGUAGE to get my ideas across!] so 'IF' you are EASILY OFFENDED or do NOT want to read anything OFFENSIVE, then please do both of us a favor and DO NOT go to my website and download this FREE gift. THANK YOU for your understanding.

CHAPTER ONE

Keep searching for products and services with the largest gap between perceived value and actual cost.

➤ These are the items that can make you rich!

➤ Look for items where the prospect doesn't know or care about your actual cost.

Keep Searching for High Value and Low Cost

Whatever you do, keep searching for products and services with the largest possible gap between the perceived value and the actual cost. Never stop doing that. **In particular, look for items where the prospects don't know or care about the cost of production.** These items can make you very rich; I know this for a fact, because this principle alone has generated tens of millions of dollars for us. It's something near and dear to my heart.

My entire life changed the day I started selling informational-based products and services. There's nothing I know of that has a higher perceived value that you can create for such a low cost, given the miracle of modern technology. **Ultimately, your actual cost has little or nothing to do with the real value that's built into such products and services.**

At the moment, we're working on something called our "Free Advertising Generator." It's included as part of a larger package, and it gives this larger package tremendous value; so in other words, it's used as a premium to help us make more sales. Just to give you an example of perceived value and actual cost, the Free Advertising Generator lets our clients give away a gift worth $687.50. **This is *real* value—something that anybody who lives in a town of over about 15,000 people can go out and purchase for $687.50—and we're letting people give it away for FREE, using the amazing miracle of technology.**

We sell it semi-blind so people don't even know what it actually is until they get involved; that helps us drive more sales.

This valuable item consists of 50 of my books that are currently for sale on the Internet through amazon.com, barnesandnoble.com, and many other Web-based bookstores. For that matter, any bookstore in your local area can order these books, because they're real, physical books made of paper. They all have ISBN numbers, and their prices total to $687.50. But thanks to modern technology, we can give them to people absolutely free, because they're all digitized and Chris Lakey has put them up on a website. And as you know, everybody loves getting a valuable free gift!

That's just one example of what you can do with modern technology. **These are real books—but in a digital form that costs zero for us to deliver them.** They never run out, either. Using the Internet, the cost of delivery is nada; **and we can arrange for other people to give them away for free, too.** The people responding to the offer don't care that the books are digital, or that it costs us nothing to reproduce and deliver them. They see the value nowadays, though for a while people didn't place as high a perceived value on purely digital products. All that's changing; people are starting to see the advantages of eBook readers and iPads, and even smartphones like iPhones have Kindle readers and similar apps you can download.

Granted, there *is* a lot of digitized stuff out there that's total trash; that's part of the reason that digitized products just didn't "smell" right to people for a long while. But they understand that our products are, in fact, real books that have simply been digitized. **There's a tremendous amount of credibility already**

built into these books, given that we sell them offline in forms that you can hold and put on a shelf; that gives them a much higher perceived value than a lot of the stuff on the Internet. Plus, people often just come up with the prices for their products out of thin air; there's nothing to substantiate those prices at all. **We** *can* **substantiate ours.**

And although we're giving the books away as a part of our Free Advertising Generator, we intend to sell the whole Advertizing Generator package itself for a lot of money. **So as you can see, a simple informational product can be quite profitable.** And incidentally—all books are informational products, whether printed or digitized. So are some forms of software, and of course seminars are classic informational products. We've charged as much as $3,000-5,000 for seminars in the past, and some people charge even more. **The more people we're able to put into those events, the cheaper they become to produce, and the more of that fee is pure profit.** You've got the fixed cost of the seminar room and preparation, the cost of the promotion, and bringing in your speakers; but the more people you can comfortably pack into that room, the lower the actual cost per person. **All you have to do is give them a great show and transmit tremendous value, so they leave feeling happy.**

The perceived value at a moneymaking seminar is high because people know they can walk away with a handful of ideas that can make them a fortune. Even one idea can make a million dollars, if played right; I know that's true because I've done it. **The potential results you're offering are huge, when compared to the price.** We call that selling money at a discount, and we've done it to the tune of millions of dollars.

Selling informational products is an exciting prospect, and it's only getting more so as new, innovative developments come along. Take the Kindle and similar devices. Back when we first started selling eBooks in the late 1990s, you had to read them on your computer. Well, you couldn't easily curl up with a good computer, and that's still not easy. But with small, portable eBook readers, you can. They've given digitized products a whole new level of acceptability and profitability—and that's only going to improve as time goes on.

Another type of information product we've sold very successfully, because they've got such a high perceived value and a relatively low delivery cost, are website bundles. We started selling websites back in 1994, along with our good friend Alan R. Bechtold, who helped us break into the website developing business. With Alan's help, we developed extremely high-value websites that were the equivalent of what other people were charging tens of thousands of dollars for—yet we sold them for under a thousand dollars. We made millions of dollars doing that.

A website is basically just software—a type of computer code—and it's tremendously valuable to those who need it, because of what it would cost them if they had to develop it on their own. **And yet, if you can sell a lot of copies of it, the cost to put a website together and replicate it is cheap in the long run, even if you have to spend a lot of money to develop it in the first place.** You can make as many copies as you like; and because the Internet is so huge, you can sell thousands of the same basic website. That drives the price way down, and nobody has to worry about competition, so you're not hurting your customers at all. The more of them you sell, the more profit you make. **Your initial cost to develop the site is quickly covered by the profits.**

Our new Health Resource Portal contains over 2,000 health resource websites—powerful moneymaking websites that other people have developed. These websites are worth a tremendous amount of money. If you had to develop the products and services they sell, and then had to write all the advertising copy and pay somebody to put these sites together, each could potentially cost hundreds or thousands of dollars to create. **We tell people that each website has a real world value of $98.79, so we've backed off on the real price somewhat. But when you take $98.79 times 2,000, you end up with $197,580... almost $200,000 worth of websites!** Even at that price, you're talking unbelievable savings, since some of these sites really would cost thousands of dollars to develop from scratch. Still, just having something that's worth almost $200,000 is already pushing the boundary of believability—especially since we sell it for under $5,000.

Remember this: what people really want is expensive, high-quality items for dirt-cheap prices. They *don't* want dirt-cheap stuff; they want valuable stuff for cheap prices. **When you're selling information products and doing your job correctly, that's what you're able to provide them.** These websites are very valuable, and part of that perceived value, of course, is the cost that you would incur if you had to pay a website developer to put it all together from scratch — especially if you didn't know what you were doing. This is an ocean that's filled with a lot of man-eating sharks who will eat you and your money up, if you're not careful. They'll take advantage of you, and you'll end up spending a whole lot more money than you'd have to spend if you knew what you were doing.

And remember, when it comes to the cost of developing websites, I'm not just talking about the web development itself. I'm also talking about the actual words you have to put on the website that make people want to give their money up in exchange for whatever it is you're selling. Good copywriting is an art and a skill that takes many years to develop, and the best copywriters charge a fortune—because they're worth it. **And yet, in the end, it doesn't matter what something costs; all that matters is how much profit it makes you. Your cost is just an investment towards future profits.**

Another part of the value of these Health Resource Portal websites is the money they make you. You've got 2,000 websites; and let's say that each one pays you an average commission of $20 every time you sell something. All you need is a few sales from a few hundred of those websites every month, and you're making thousands of dollars monthly. **And the marketing system not only runs by itself, all the fulfillment of the products is taken care of, and the customer service nightmares are handled by others.** Because it's a completely hands-off type of business, you can put in just a few minutes a day running it—while making a huge amount of money. Needless to say, that also affects the perceived value.

It took Chris Lakey many, many months to put all this together, and as of this writing, **it still has to go through some beta testing before all the bugs are completely worked out.**

18

But once they are, the cost to reproduce it is basically nil. It's sort of like the Hollywood movie business. Sure, in Hollywood it may cost them $50 million to shoot a movie, and that's before they take in their first dollar. But if they do their marketing right, they can make all their money back in one weekend. Any money that comes in after that is pure gravy. After its theater run worldwide—which may last up to a year—it goes into DVD and pay-per-view, and there's all kinds of other ways to make money via licensing and such. So who cares how much it cost to make, when you can be drowning in profits after it's introduced? **Selling information products allows you to do the same thing—and they cost even less to reproduce than films do.**

Simply put, selling information products can make you very, very wealthy. Here at M.O.R.E., Inc., we've been doing it since the late 1980s; and since then, there have been numerous technological advancements that have made doing it even easier. **The average person now has a much better chance of making money at this than we had when we got started. It's exciting, hugely profitable, and it allows you to give people tremendous value.** I just gave you an example where our customers are getting almost $200,000 in value for something we're selling for under $5,000. And not only do they get the websites, but we're also throwing in a whole bunch of other extremely valuable items in the same package. And you know what? People are just going *crazy* for this. Customers love it. Everyone's happy, and everybody is making money.

And think about that: **the digital age we're living in has made it so that a lot more people have opportunities to make a lot of money.** It's revolutionized the business of information selling, as well as many other marketplaces—including moviemaking. Obviously, the movie industry is much different than ours; but when you get right down to it, a movie is just information, delivered in a specific format that people watch because they feel it will offer some value to them— entertainment, at the very least. So the film companies make movies to appeal to their target audiences: romantic comedies for the ladies, action flicks for the men and teen boys, and the like. And while traditionally they're delivered in movie theaters, you can now get movies on DVDs or streamed through Netflix, Amazon, or a similar online provider. Most movies are now basically digital products.

Similarly, musicians try to produce music that's pleasing to the ear, according to their audience. They too take advantage of new advances in technology to decrease their costs and deliver their products. **Cassette tapes are cheaper to produce than vinyl LPs, and CDs are cheaper than both;** and the industry moved to those cheaper delivery formats when they had the chance. Who knows what cheap format we'll all deliver our products on in a decade or two?

It's the same thing with books. **Books are the classic information products,** and they come in a wide variety of subject matter, both fiction and non-fiction. Traditionally, they're distributed through books and libraries, but advances in information technology have allowed their distribution via eBook readers like the Kindle, and that's taken off dramatically. **That decreases the cost of production, while maintaining high value for the customer.** As with movies, music, and just about every other mode of information delivery, the digital revolution has allowed profitable changes in the way books are delivered and consumed.

Some people have serious hang-ups with digital products—and sometimes, that's just nuts. Now, you can say, "I'm not comfortable with digital technology. Maybe I'm not a computer person. That kind of scares me a little," and that's perfectly fine. But don't tell me that digital products aren't real, or that a product isn't valid because it doesn't have a physical existence independent of the machine you listen to, watch, or read it on. **The format doesn't really matter. The actual quality is based on the content of the product, not its delivery vehicle.** Just because you watch a film on a computer six weeks after its release in theaters doesn't mean it's bad because you didn't see it in a theater. If it's bad, it's bad, no matter what format you watch it on.

Sure, you may miss a few nuances (and overpriced popcorn) by not seeing a movie in a theater. But convenience, and numerous other advantages, can outweigh what you've missed. You can watch a movie on a computer three or four different ways; and besides that, you can watch it on your TV via pay-per-view. You can even download movies on your Play Station 3, iPod, iPad, smartphone, or TiVo. You've got options unheard of five years ago!

However you watch it, it's that same movie that cost $50 million to make. It's the same movie you could buy or rent on DVD. Now you can buy that same exact content in digital form. **Maybe that requires a slight shift in the way you think about digital information... but still, it's the same content, and that's what makes it so powerful.** If the studios would just wrap their minds around this (and they haven't completely, yet), they would realize that they can make greater profits because they can deliver things for much less cost than ever before. You might recall that it took them a long time to get comfortable with the idea of home video in the first place. When videotapes first came out, they charged huge prices for them—partly because they hated the idea of a form of distribution they didn't completely control. But they came around; and while they're bucking the digital trend a bit today, they'll come around on that, too.

It's the same with music. You don't even have to buy music on a CD anymore; you can just download it for your computer or digital music player via iTunes or Amazon. Some services allow you to stream music content just like you do movies. **As for books—well, apparently more digital books are sold than new printed books nowadays.**

So as you can see, information products have changed drastically as a result of the digital revolution. It's the same content delivered in a different kind of package—a package that, for an entrepreneur, is cheaper to deliver. The digital revolution has made it possible for many entrepreneurs in the information business to make much more money than they used to. So don't get hung up on the way that the content is delivered; focus on the content. The content is all that matters.

I can recall a small booklet less than 100 pages long that one entrepreneur sold by mail for $1,000. He told people flat-out that there were no refunds; but plenty of people bought it anyway, because the content was so valuable to them. It just goes to show that people will pay huge amounts of money for quality content, no matter how it's presented. **If you're in the right marketplace, and people are hungry for good-quality information, you can deliver that information in any number of ways, and still get people to buy it.**

I've pointed out that you have to look for items where the prospect doesn't know or care about your actual cost. Well, in a lot of industries, especially those where the products are commoditized, people are highly sensitive about what things cost to produce, and they basically know what that cost should be. Take gasoline, for example. You might go to the pump and see that the cost is $3.00. Most people realize that there's not much markup on gasoline, once you get past the taxes the government makes you add. So generally, the gas station isn't making much money on gas; they're hoping you come into the store and spend money there.

People have a general idea about how much profit there is or should be in a tank of gas, because it's a commodity. It's the same thing with any supply-and-demand type of product. Most consumers have a kind of financial radar, and if they *have* to buy something, they know how much it should cost; so they're on the lookout for the best possible deal and the cheapest form of delivery. **Whereas with information products, especially those directed to a targeted niche marketplace, prospects don't really care how much it costs to produce and deliver. They only care about what it will do for them.**

Let's say I had a simple, proven cure for cancer, and I could easily write the formula on a paper napkin. What would that napkin, which might cost half a cent to make, then be worth? Does the form of delivery matter in a case like this? Obviously, the napkin is priceless to a person suffering from cancer, or for a member of their family. **It's the quality of the information that matters, *not* the way it's delivered.**

I could also record that cancer formula on an audio program and create a CD of the recording. What's a CD worth? Intrinsically, less than a buck for that piece of mass-produced plastic and metal foil. Now, when a CD has music on it, it's valued at $10-20. Even if it's the latest and greatest from your favorite band, you're not going to pay much more than that for it; only a real fanatic would spring for, say, $100 for a regular CD. If it contains certain forms of information, then sure, those who need it or otherwise value it highly might pay that much. But if that CD provides a genuine, effective formula for a cancer cure, would it be worth $1,000? Probably. Would it be worth $5,000? I would suspect so. **A single CD containing certain information becomes tremendously valuable to the person who needs that information, just as a million-dollar idea written in ballpoint on a McDonald's napkin is still worth $1,000,000.**

So don't get too hung up on the format or vehicle of distribution. It's the content that's important. If you can find content that people really want, they'll pay more attention to the content than the price—which will lead to a situation where they really don't care what the actual costs to produce and duplicate the information are. They don't care what that sheet of paper cost; they care what's printed on the sheet of paper. They don't care what that CD costs; they care what's on the CD when they pop it in their CD player. They don't care that you're paying $19.95 a month for web hosting; they only want the product you're going to download to them. *People really don't care about how you get the information to them if the information is valuable to them.*

You do, of course. **That's why you have to keep searching for products and services with the biggest possible gap between the perceived value and the actual cost, so you can maximize your profit margins.** That's the formula for success here: quality content delivered in the least expensive way possible. Don't be too cheap, of course, or the quality of the distribution format may turn some folks off; but you don't have to inscribe it on gold tablets or deliver it in calligraphy on the finest parchment, either. Let me re-emphasize that what people *really* want is tremendous value for the lowest possible price. Who wouldn't pay $100 for a genuine $5,000 Rolex?

Plenty of people are making fortunes by catering to this desire in the information marketing field. If you want to emulate them, then model your behavior after theirs. Buy their products, and look at how they're handling their delivery, then put those methods into play yourself. **Keep your eye out for new ways to delivery your information even more cheaply.** Once you get some experience under your belt, you'll be able to branch out on your own with new ideas that make this method even more effective.

CHAPTER TWO

Customers go where they are invited **and stay where they are appreciated.**

Customers Go Where They're Invited—and Stay Where They're Appreciated

Customers go where they are invited and stay where they are appreciated. **Think hard about this one, because in a general sense at least, it's the foundation of all business.** It sounds like common sense, doesn't it? But as Mark Twain pointed out more than a century ago, common sense is a very uncommon thing. Human nature hasn't really changed since then.

Why don't more businesspeople and marketers seem to understand this principal? Why don't they do a better job of inviting and re-inviting their customers to come back and see them more often? Why don't they express their appreciation to existing customers more openly and more often, and simply do the best they can to consistently provide good value? That's hard to say; **but it seems almost as if a lot of the people in the business arena just toss aside some of the basic values that they learned at their mother's knee—including the famous Golden Rule—and don't bother with basic marketing methods at all.**

If you collect the right information, it's not that hard to go back to existing customers and invite them to buy more of what they bought from you the first time. If you do that and don't see an effect, invite them more often. **Stay in touch with them on a regular basis.** So many businesspeople *do not do that.* They wait for the customers to come to them; and maybe the assumption that people *will* come to them when they need what the market has to offer forms the basis of this self-deluding behavior. Maybe they just don't do it because it requires some effort that they feel they can't spare. **Whatever the case, most business people just aren't proactively and aggressively trying to get people to come back again and again.**

To keep customers coming back, you've got to prove to them that you *do* appreciate them; and in order to do that, you have to understand your customers at the most intimate level. I've said this over and over throughout this book, and it's especially true with this particular facet of business operation. And again, it's not that difficult to do this. Once you've pinpointed whatever it is your customers really want, you've got the basic premise that allows you to offer your customers things that make them want to do business with you repeatedly.

I'm sure that there may be some exceptions to this, **but for the most part, the only way you're ever going to get rich in business is by attracting repeat customers. That doesn't happen without a lot of work.** Oh, a few people may come back on their own; but as a rule they do not. You've got to work at this, just like everything else.

Now, to some people, giving people more of what they bought from you the first time (the basis of this principal) may sound like the opposite of common sense... because once they've solved their problem, why do they need more? Well, first of all, people in most marketplaces are insatiable. They're always going to want to buy more than you can produce. You've got to pound that idea into your head and drill it into your brain: *your customers always want far more than you can actually produce,* **as long as you're consistently producing good value and providing the results they want.** In fact, if that's the case, you're doing them a disservice if you're *not* trying to sell them more of what they bought the first time. In addition to being insatiable, people want to do business with people they like and they trust, people that they feel have their best interests at heart.

Here's a quick story to illustrate the point: Randy Hamilton, the bookkeeper/accountant at our parent company, started with us in the late 1980s—so he's been with us for decades now. He knew quite a bit about business when he first came onboard, given his education and experience. Back then, our business was booming, despite the fact that we were a brand new company, barely a year old... and he couldn't understand why. He took a good look at our product line, decided that it left a lot to be desired, and thought we didn't have much of a future. He told himself right then and there: "Man, I've got to get my resume out there! This company is not going to last."

But then he got busy and forgot about it. Every few weeks, he'd surface and say to himself, "Man, I need to take off a little early this week so I can get my resume out there—because this company isn't going to last." **To make a long story short, he kept saying that to himself the first year or two, truly believing there was no possible way that a company that sold the kind of things we did could make it long-term. The punchline is that over 20 years later, he's still here, and we're more successful than ever.**

Randy is a very smart guy; as a Mensa member, his IQ is off the charts. And he had a good formal education and significant experience, so he knew something about business

31

when he joined us. **But he didn't understand the insatiability of a rabid marketplace like the one that we're in — the fact that people just** *cannot* **get enough.** Because of that, they'll keep coming back and buying more of what they bought the first time, as long as they're well treated and what we offer is somewhat different from what they've bought before.

There's a seeming paradox there, you may have noticed; **people want more of what they bought before, but they want it to be new.** That's a real phenomenon, and it's why marketers should always think about what's next. People are addicted to "new." **But what they're really after is the benefits behind your products or services.** If you can provide those effectively, then the original purchase will often fuel the desire for more purchases. To put it in a memorable way, it stokes the fires of their desires.

If you don't try to sell new things to them after you've stoked those fires, then guess what? They're going to go get the benefits they want from somebody else. If you're an ambitious person and you want to make the most money you can, that idea should drive you a little crazy. **You don't want the customers that** *you* **spent money to acquire, the people** *you* **worked hard to build relationships with, to go spend their money with a competitor.** If that doesn't upset you just a little, then you should crank up the volume on your ambition level. Take a good, hard look at what you're really trying to do here, because they're *your* customers and they should be spending that money with *you*... not your competitors! **So always think about what's next, realizing that people want more of whatever they bought from you the first time with a slightly different twist.**

Here at M.O.R.E., Inc., one of the things we do is develop websites for our clients. We build or find the right websites that sell the products and services they want, we develop the marketing systems that make it all a cohesive unit, and we give people an automatic turnkey way to make money with those websites with a minimum of their own input. As follow-ups to those products, in keeping with this idea that we have to develop more of what they bought from us the first time, we create bigger website packages that offer them more profit potential. **More, more, more—always give them more.** People are addicted to new stuff. They crave it.

We live in a consumer-oriented society; and again, **the purchases that people make stoke the fires of their desire.** That makes them want to buy even more. **That's why you've always got to come up with something new, and why you've got to stay in touch with your customers to let them know about your new products.** You've got to repeatedly re-invite them to come back for more; and in doing so, you've got to make them feel appreciated. Therefore, do all you can to continually build mutually beneficial relationships with customers, constantly looking for ways to get them to want to do more business with you.

My favorite metaphor for this process is restaurants. In a way, we're all in the restaurant business. With few exceptions, restaurants can only survive if they get people to come back and spend their money on a regular basis. We all have our favorite restaurants—and they depend on that tendency. Recently, I went to one of my favorite restaurants that I hadn't visited for a long time, because it's a little bit out of the way from where I live.

Yet even though I hadn't been in there for well over a year, they made this special dish just for me—or at least, that's how they made me feel. And that's the whole secret of the restaurant business: you have to make people feel special. That night, the owner came out and shook my hand, his son came out and said hi to me, and they made this little dish for me. **I didn't even ask for it; they just made it and brought it to the table.**

That's what a good restaurant does. The people who run it know that the secret to their success is to get people to keep coming back, and to tell their friends and family, who will throw parties and bring groups there, and will ideally ask them to do the catering when they have a big event. It's all a part of giving the customer more, more, more, so they'll buy more stuff, more often, for more profit. **You've got to keep re-inviting them, and you've got to show them they're appreciated.** Do it properly, and the question is not, "Will you get rich?" The question is, "How rich will you get, and when will you get all that money?"

This is one of those basic principles that should govern *all* businesses. The entrepreneurs who get it right tend to do well; the ones that don't tend to fail. **It all comes down to how people feel about doing business with you.** It has to do with the reaction they get when they're in your store, at your restaurant, visiting your website, or talking to you on the phone. Customers will go where they're invited, and will stay where they're appreciated.

Too many business owners assume that if they're open, people are going to find their businesses automatically. I call this the "if you build it they will come" mentality. They feel no need to advertise, so they don't do anything to attract customers—and then they wonder why they don't have any. Well, again, customers go where they're invited. So ask them! **Tell them who you are, what you do, and invite them to come visit you. That's Business 101.** Let your marketplace know you exist, and invite them to do business with you by making an attractive offer. Be aggressive about it.

If you run a retail store, you want people to know who you are, where you are, and why you're there. They learn those things through the promotions that you run. Why should they just be able to pick it up out of the air? They've got so many other things competing for their attention. **You have to make people pay attention to you and want to interact with you.** You have to make them feel appreciated because you're actually making the effort to get them to do business with you.

Passive, hopeful, word-of-mouth marketing is all very well and good, and you may get some business that way when people hear about or stumble onto you; but it doesn't really cut it these days, not if you want to really compete and maximize your market share. **No, you have to aggressively go after that business, no matter what kind of business you run.** With few exceptions, people just aren't going to come to you unless you invite them in and make them feel welcome.

Look at your personal life. It's one thing to hang out with people in public places; but if you don't invite them to your home, most of them won't ever come by unless they need something from you, or just happen to be in the area. People are busy; they have their own lives going on, so absent an invitation to remind them you're there and that you welcome your attention, they probably won't bother to visit. **It's easy to see how this applies to business as well.**

You know, I'll occasionally go to Wal-Mart because I have to pick up some basic necessity, and I know that I can get it there at a decent price. But there are a lot of other places in town that I'm never going to go to unless I'm invited. I don't even think about them, because they've never bothered to remind me that they're there, and that they've got some of the things I need. I'm not inclined to visit those stores just because they exist (even if I know they do), so the marketing they do to attract me is their only hope of getting me in their doors. **Even if I'm a good prospect for what they sell, unless they've invited me and made me feel like I'm welcome, I've got no reason to visit them.**

This is even truer if you're dealing with a national marketplace. If a business is located in another state, the only way they're likely to attract you and keep your business is by continue inviting you to do business with them—by email, mail, phone, or whatever. If they don't keep inviting you, and letting you know that they really appreciate your business, you're going to go somewhere else for that product or service. **Constant marketing contact and communication is a must. Don't see it as an expense, but as a practical necessity if you expect to maximize your profits.** And if you don't expect that, why are you in business in the first place?

Once you have a customer, you don't want to let them go. Now, in a free market economy, you can't physically keep people from doing business with your competitors, so all you can do is encourage them to choose you over anyone else. When your customers feel appreciated, there's more reason for them to stay with you instead of wondering off. **People tend to stay in business relationships where they feel important and wanted.** That's just human nature. So it's not enough just to keep bringing new customers in; you've got to keep your existing customers happy and appreciated.

Beyond repeated invitations to do business with you, you can try to retain customers by implement things like customer appreciation sales or discounts, or loyalty programs designed to reward people for being good customers. **Even simple things like personalized mailings and appreciative language in your communications can help.** Very few people feel especially appreciated if your communications are addressed to "Dear Friend," "Occupant," or "Addressee." When it's obvious that you've sent something to everybody in the zip code, the recipients just feel like numbers. How is that going to help you? So instead, call them by their name: "Dear John" or "Dear Betty." Refer to them as a "preferred customer," and make them feel special. Tell them you have a nice sale on specifically for them. **Anything you can do to make them feel appreciated will help them decide that there's no other place they would rather do business with.**

People tend to be creatures of habit, and very comfortable with the status quo. It's hard to get most people to change... unless they're ticked off at you. If a business has done you wrong, you're more likely to leave, right? So don't let that happen. **Do things to make folks feel special, and do your best not to offend them.** Continuously let them know that you welcome their business and appreciate them as customers, so they'll stick around and you can continue offering them new or related products and services.

So, let's recap this. **Part One: Customers go where they're invited. Part Two: Let those customers know they're appreciated, and they'll stick around. It's a simple formula for wealth.** Most companies aren't doing this, which gives you a competitive advantage. So do what most people aren't; and when you do find the occasional company that has figured this out and is profiting enormously by it, emulate them. Follow the leaders, do your best to improve on what they're doing here, and eventually *you'll* be a leader. **Do a phenomenal job of inviting and re-inviting customers to do business with you, give them what they want the most, and show a deep appreciation for them.**

It's a very simple idea, and yet it can earn you all the money you'll ever want or need.

CHAPTER THREE

After a while, you <u>STOP</u> listening to what other people say — and *only* pay attention to what they do.

Stop Listening to What Other People Say, and Only Pay Attention to What They Do

As my Grandma Clara always used to say, the only way to really know somebody is by the actions that they take. She was absolutely right in that regard. **Many people talk a mean game, but only by observing their actions can you truly know who and what they are.**

For example: back in 1990, we bought the company Profit Ideas from Russ von Hoelscher and George Sterne. Russ had been running a full-page ad for a number of years, where he was offering a booklet for just one dollar (for shipping and handling) as a lead-in to a bigger sale, and that ad was always profitable for him. As part of the purchase price of the company, we got that same full-page ad. Well, I was young and rebellious at the time, and I thought I knew more than Russ did. So I figured, "Well, maybe that dollar is slowing down the flow of the leads. Let's just offer the book completely free."

So I re-did the ad, taking out that dollar qualifier, and re-ran it. Sure enough, we soon doubled the amount of leads coming in—and I was feeling so righteous, so cocky, so arrogant! I thought that *I* was right, and Russ was wrong. But in the end, that ad didn't make a profit. **We had the increased cost of sending out all those booklets, but we weren't able to convert enough of those leads to sales to make it worth the cost.**

Now, just asking for a dollar doesn't sound like a lot;

everybody has a buck in their wallet. **But remember, it's the actions that people take that matter; that's the only way that you can tell anything about a person.** That one dollar made all the difference in the world, because it separated out the people who were serious about the offer from everyone else. Even if it's just a dollar, when people pay, they pay attention. Remember that. Even though Russ was only asking them to pay a dollar, the respondents took his ad more seriously, he attracted a better-qualified prospective buyer, and ultimately Russ was right and we were wrong.

Nowadays, we often ask for a small amount of money on our initial lead generation offers. We could just give away the offer for free... and for our very best customers, that's what we sometimes do. There's no need for any qualification there; those people have already qualified themselves. **But if someone has never done any business with us before, we ask for a little money upfront** because, again, just because somebody is on a list of prime prospects and they claim they're serious about the kinds of things we sell, that doesn't mean they actually are. Since the only way you can really tell if they're serious is by the actions they take, we get them to spend some money.

We've got a new strategy we're trying right now; I call it our "bad mailing list strategy." **We're trying to make good profits from bad mailing lists, with the understanding that there are a lot more marginal mailing lists than there are good ones.** They're *almost* good enough, but not quite. **Well, sometimes, all you have to do to make them better is charge more money.** When you do that, the very best prospects identify themselves, because they're willing to spend that money. That may seem counterintuitive, but it really works, because it separates the valuable wheat from the chaff. Basically, that's the foundation of the entire two-step marketing strategy anyway. STEP #1 is asking people to take a small step, to do something simple to qualify themselves. Then and only then do you come in with STEP #2, in which you try to convert that lead into a sale, and then that sale into a repeat buyer. **Two-step marketing is the safest form of marketing. The first step is *always* to get people to qualify themselves by taking specific action.**

This concept of judging people by their actions works in all aspects of business, not just with prospective customers. Here's a good example: a technique used by the late James Tollison, who helped me get started back in the mid-1980s. James promoted a multi-level marketing opportunity, and he'd have seminars in out-of-the-way locations where people really had to work to get there. **His theory was that only the most serious people were going to show up. I think that's an excellent way of qualifying prospects.**

We're going to San Diego later this year to do a seminar, and we're probably only going to have enough people at the event to bring a couple of our very best salespeople with us. So who will those salespeople be? Well, our sales manager, Drew Hansen, has a sales contest every year; this year, it's during our fourth annual Branson seminar. Those who sell the most at that event are the ones who get to go to San Diego. Again, what counts are actions and results. **It's easy to gauge who's genuinely serious in a sales environment, based on the number of sales they're making.** Admittedly, it's a little harder to do in other environments; but start paying attention to people's actions, because doing so can be very profitable.

I'm very, very proud of the core group I've surrounded myself with. I've learned how they react in stressful situations, when things don't go right—or worse, when *nothing* goes right. Remember, that's the only way you can really judge someone's character, and understand what they're all about and who they are. And conversely, people are watching you, too, to see how you react—never forget that. **If you're in any kind of a leadership position, people are *always* watching your actions, waiting to see what happens when everything goes wrong.** They're especially eager to see what happens when you make a mistake. So be aware of that, and tread cautiously.

And keep in mind that your very best customers—the people who spend the most money with you—have to be separated from everyone else. Their actions help you filter them out. The 80/20 rule asserts that 80% of your profits will come from 20% of your customers (sometimes it's more like 90/10). **This is a very real phenomenon, which is why you need to keep a sharp eye on what people are buying, so you can let the best buyers qualify themselves.** Once you've got a qualified prospect, you can be very aggressive in your marketing, because they've proven they're seriously interested in what you're selling.

Now you can afford to spend a bunch of money to chase after them and do the kinds of things necessary to convert them. You simply can't do that without qualifying them first; otherwise, you're likely to go broke. You always have to apply very specific marketing strategies intended to separate out the smaller, serious group of people from all the rest. **The larger**

the action you require of them, the better they qualify themselves. This is true whether you're asking them to spend money or jump through a hoop in some other way; for example, you might have them listen to a long message and then call a phone number. Only the truly committed will do that.

Once you've determined who's willing to overcome these obstacles, you can go after them aggressively, spending more freely than you would on lesser prospects. You do have to be smart about it, of course; your margins must be good, and you still have to track everything, but you can be more assertive in trying to convert those leads to sales. **Aggressive marketing is part of the secret to getting rich—and you can't be aggressive with your marketing until and unless you do things that force your prospects to show you whether they're serious or not.**

Strangely enough, the well-qualified people who become your very best customers tend to cause you the fewest problems in the long run. I've seen this in action myself. The reverse is also true: the customers who spend the least, or buy from you least often, are the source of a large majority of your customer service issues. Typically, this is because the people who spend the least money just want to wring the biggest advantage out of you that they can. They're looking for a "deal" of some kind, or they want something for nothing... and they cause trouble when they don't get it. They don't take into account the fact that they have, in fact, gotten a good deal, and should back off on their expectations, given the amount of money they've paid.

Customers who have spent more on a project tend to be

more engaged than other clients in any case, and have clearer expectations of exactly what they're looking for. Even if they do turn out to be more demanding or urgent, you're willing to accept that, because they *have* paid you more money for it. You're also willing to accept more frequent interaction, because they've paid for the privilege.

And that's the whole point here. This brings together a couple of sayings we've all heard before: **"Talk is cheap," and "Actions speak louder than words." These are clichés because they're so true.** It's easy to say anything, and lots of people do—they spout whatever comes to mind regarding their intentions, and they'll give you all kinds of assurances, and then many times won't follow through with what they've said. Therefore, actions really do speak louder than words. If you say you'll do something for me, I appreciate the fact that you've said that; but what I appreciate more is having you come to me and tell me it's done.

Chris Lakey has six kids, and he tells me that if he just proceeded on the assumption that anything they said they'd do would get done—whether that involved taking out the trash, or doing laundry, or putting toys away—then his household would be run quite differently. But even with kids, talk is cheap; so Chris says he's always getting onto the kids and having to remind them that when they say that they're going to do something, they need to follow through. So while the 13-year-old always says that he'll clean up after himself when he takes a shower, and he usually does remember, there might be one or two times a week when he forgets and needs to be reminded. Chris and his wife appreciate his actions more than they appreciate his words... because again, talk is cheap. **As always, the follow-through, the actual action, says more about a person than what they tell you.**

In the world of business and marketing, people often just say what they think you want to hear. This is true in most of your life, actually. Think about your casual conversations. You might walk up to someone and say, "How's it going?" and they'll probably say, "Great! Fine!" or something similar. Usually, that isn't *really* how things are going. They're just telling you what they think you want to hear... and basically, they want to hear the same from you. If you actually told someone, "You know what, I'm having a horrible day and here are the reasons why... Do you have an hour to listen?," they might turn around and run. They certainly weren't planning on you saying that. All they wanted was a platitude, and that's all they wanted to give you.

If you go into a clothing store and start flipping through the racks, and a sales clerk comes over to ask if they can help you with anything, what do you say most of the time? "Just looking..." Well, how many people really *are* just looking? Occasionally that may be the case, but usually it's just what people say, true or not.

People have all kinds of reasons for doing this—but mostly they respond as they do because it's easy. If, as a marketer, you ask someone if they want a benefit you're offering, it's easy for them to tell you yes. For example: if you ask a room full of overweight people, "How many of you would like to lose weight?", all of them are going to say yes. If you ask a room full of entrepreneurs if they want to make money, well, of course they do. But the question is, how hard are they willing to work to achieve that benefit? What kinds of actions are they willing to take? **Remember, a person's actions matter much more than what they say. Words are a dime a dozen, if they're worth that much.** It's easy for people to verbalize the things they want. "I want a new car." "I want to be happier." "I want to be skinnier." "I want to do this..." "I want to do that..."

If you ask your group of would-be entrepreneurs, "How many of you would be willing to actually buy a business?", or "How many of you would be willing to take out a bank loan to finance a new start-up?", the number of takers will be drastically reduced. Similarly, if you ask the overweight group, "How many of you would commit to walking five miles a day to lose weight?", very few will raise their hands. **Whatever the action is, requiring an action automatically reduces the number of people willing to commit to it.** It's one thing to say something; it's another to do it. So as a marketer, you have to ignore what people say and turn your attention to what they actually do. Move beyond words and into actions.

Back when we first started promoting the Profit Ideas book, we set it up so people could get it for free just by asking. They didn't have to send us a cent first; all they had to do was verbalize that they wanted it. There was no cost or commitment... so they weren't serious about moving on to the next step. It was too easy. We ultimately discovered that while charging a dollar caused the response to drop, the quality of leads was much higher. People qualified themselves with that dollar. Those leads turned into customers more often because they had something on the table—because they took an action.

So, to repeat: generally, requiring an action is going to get you a better, more qualified prospect.

You can tweak the required action as necessary, depending on your offer and marketing model. In some instances, we've required actions that were very easy to take, like spending a dollar. In other cases, we've required actions that cost as much as $40 or more. **Really, all we were looking for was for someone to raise their hand and put a little money on the line, to give us something beyond just a verbal nod to show they were interested in taking a positive step toward their own betterment.**

People don't necessarily have to spend money to take an action. You can have them take action by filling out a survey or questionnaire to show their interest; or, as I mentioned earlier, you can have them listen to a long telephone presentation. Or, you can have them make a sort of delayed payment; for example, you might ask for their credit card number and say, "We won't bill you now. We'll bill you in 30 days, if you like what you receive." In a case like this, they put their money on the line, even though you're not going to charge them right away (if at all). We've had offers where we've had prospects write post-dated checks; we told them, "We won't cash your check for 30 days. You have a full month to check it all out; if you don't like it, just let us know and we'll return your check or shred it. Your choice." By actually mailing a check, they've taken an action, even if they ultimately decide they don't want what we have to offer.

Again, actions speak so much louder than words. **Never lose sight of the fact that people will often talk a good game**

without intending to actually follow through with action. You can get verbal commitments out of people for all kinds of things. Consider the issue of fundraiser pledges. People often commit to pledge a certain amount of money, either monthly or all at once, and then don't keep their promises. If you've ever listened to public radio, you've probably had to suffer through the fundraisers they're forced to put on every six months or so. One reason they have to keep doing so is that some people who pledge simply don't follow through with the donations they've promised, so the station is forced to plead for more donations. Even so, I'm sure they try to plan it into their budget and into their marketing, because **the harsh truth is that people usually won't put their money where their mouth is.** If you're letting people verbally commit to something, you know that a percentage of them won't follow through.

We've done something similar with live events. We have several a year, in which we host clients from all over the country. Some fly in, some drive in long-distance, and some are local. We can almost guarantee that if our event is free, only a fraction of the people who tell us they're going to show up actually do. We count on that to some extent, because we know that's how people are. **Ah, but if you ask people to take an action, if they have to put money on the table, they're more likely to follow through.** By committing at a higher level, they're going to turn into better customers.

In business, that's the name of the game! **So make people commit. Make them take an action… and the more actions they have to take, the better.** If they have to spend money, return a form, visit your website, or make a phone call, then they're qualifying themselves, showing you they're serious. **Remember: as long as you've got a really good, qualified prospect, and your profit margins are good, then you have the golden key that lets you become extremely aggressive with your marketing.** Aggressive marketing is the factor that separates the most successful companies and entrepreneurs from everyone else. But it's expensive to market aggressively, and the money has to come from somewhere; which is why you need to focus on that small group of imminently qualified prospects.

It all starts with pre-qualifying your prospective buyers, and providing a product or service that has a high profit margin built in, so that you can afford to spend more money on your marketing. **So stop listening to what people say, and force them to take action. That's all that matters in the long run.**

CHAPTER FOUR

Think of the groups of leads you attract into your business as a HUGE TON of dirt, mud, and rocks — <u>with</u> <u>a</u> <u>few</u> <u>solid</u> <u>gold</u> <u>nuggets</u> mixed in with all this filth! Your job is to keep sifting through all the mud and crap to find these gold nuggets!

You must sift through this rubble in the cheapest possible way — so the <u>majority</u> of your marketing costs can be invested in the gold nugget group — not the muddy group!

Mine for Those Gold Nuggets!

Sometimes, it helps to think of each group of leads that you attract into your business as a huge pile of dirt, mud, and rocks, with a few gold nuggets mixed in. **Your job as a marketer is to sift through all the junk to find those nuggets.** And of course, you've got to be able to do so in the cheapest possible way, so you can invest the majority of your marketing costs in those rare gold nuggets rather than in the mass of material surrounding them.

That's a good visual metaphor for what we do, and it hearkens back to prospectors who pan for gold. They have to work through a lot of sand, mud, and muck to find their nuggets. The same goes for diamonds. There's a great movie called *Blood Diamond* that offers some excellent behind-the-scenes information about the diamond industry in Africa and the average life of a diamond miner; it's worth renting the DVD just to see that feature. The documentary (and the movie itself) clearly illustrate the incredible amount of dirt and rocks those diamond miners have to go through in order to find their little gems.

We marketers are also looking for the gems and nuggets among the dross. **We're mining for those customers who will spend the largest amount of money over the longest period of time, for the highest profit.** The only way to find them is by doing your initial marketing in such a way that you separate them out from much larger groups of unqualified prospects—the unprofitable ore, if you will. Now, realize that this is just an analogy; it's not a judgment on the people who don't do business with you. The point is, we're all looking for our diamonds; and in business, the best way to find them is to get them to do things to qualify themselves.

At the moment, I'm putting together a new opportunity where the very best of our customers could potentially spend as much as $100,000 with us. Ideally, the market is huge—because we're looking for would-be investors, and there are tens of millions of those in the market. By no means will more than a tiny percentage be willing to invest with us, but you have to start somewhere: so that huge marketplace is the massive amount of rock and soil in which the gold nuggets or diamonds (your choice of a metaphor) are hidden. **We'd got to do things to separate the relatively small number of good prospects from all the rest.** We've got to screen and rescreen and wash away the extraneous material. This could start with something as simple as an inexpensive book or audio program that we use to introduce people to our new investment strategy.

If someone buys that, we'll follow-up with other products and services, and thereby try to induce them to take further action to qualify themselves; and eventually, that will narrow down the field until we find the people who are most likely to ultimately give us $10,000-$100,000. Once we identify them, we can market to them more aggressively, and do even more things to qualify them and guarantee their interest. **Ironically, as the field narrows, and we can spend more on each prospect, our choices become greater.** Our power increases, because they've proven by their actions that they're very interested in what we have to offer.

We're also involved in another new opportunity where the good news and the bad news are one and the same. **The good news is that there are tens of millions of potential customers out there.** An examination of the broad demographic and psychographics of the marketplace proves that. But that's also the downside. **We may have to work our way through hundreds or thousands of prospects before we find one who will buy from us at a profit.** But we can't market aggressively and fully to all those tens of millions of people without going broke, so we have to do something to economically induce the tiny group of good prospects to separate themselves from everyone else. That's the goal of all two-step marketing.

There are plenty of ways you can do this, whether they involve sending inexpensive front-end offers to mailing lists (which already consist of people you know have bought similar things), or placing advertisements on TV, on the radio, or in magazines. **Once you dig through the leads and find those few, highly qualified prospects, you can spend more money on each of them individually, and become quite aggressive with your marketing.**

If you find it distasteful to think of your general marketplace as a mass of sludge that you have to dig through in order to find a few good customers, then **consider your marketing efforts as a kind of funnel. You have to constantly keep it full of brand new prospects, which you then process through in a series of steps that winnows the field down to a more appropriate number that you can profitably deal with.**

To do that, you need to begin with some kind of low-cost or no-cost front-end product or service to attract and acquire new customers. It has to relate closely to whatever it is you ultimately want to sell to people; I call this the "chip off the old block" principle.

So let's go back to this new investment opportunity we're putting together here at M.O.R.E., Inc. We're asking people to invest anywhere from $10,000-$100,000 with us. But you can't just step out into the marketplace and sell something like that in one go; you might get a few takers, but they'll be few and far between. In order to sell the maximum number of that sort of product, you have to sell people a chip off the old block, and then keep moving them along through the buying process until they're comfortable enough with you that you can ask them for the big bucks. **By that point, you know they're serious, and they know they can trust you. You've established a solid relationship that makes it easier for you to acquire the kind of money you're asking for.**

So keep your funnel full. Always have some kind of front-end marketing strategy in place that generates a continual flow of fresh leads. That ton of leads represents the mound of rocks that you have to go through in order to find the profitable nuggets of good, well-qualified prospects. **Do yourself a favor here and do your best to internalize that mental analogy.** If you're having trouble doing that, rent a copy of *Blood Diamond* with all the DVD extras, and watch that behind-the-scenes feature that shows you the life of a diamond miner—and all the rock, mud, filth, and sludge they have to go through in order to find those diamonds. Then try to translate that into a marketing model for your own products and services.

Chris Lakey tells me that back when he was a kid, he and his family took a trip to Cripple Creek, Colorado. Nowadays it's a casino town, but back then he and his family went mining for gold at a little creek, where they gave you a pan that you could use to sift through the rocks and dirt in search of bits of gold. Now, that was just a touristy thing; Chris and his family didn't find anything, and quite likely no one has found anything much for years. But like the *Blood Diamond* example, it's a good illustrative metaphor of what you have to do to find that tiny percentage of profitable leads in a commercial marketplace. Gold and diamonds are very hard to find in the best of circumstances, which is part of what makes them valuable; the same is true of really good business prospects. But as Chris learned back then, you'll also occasionally turn up some fool's gold. **To filter the real thing from the false, you have to keep winnowing down your pool of prospects.**

Recently, Chris says, he saw a TV show that reminded him of this experience in a dramatic way. Miners were using huge backhoe-like machines to dredge the shallow waters off the coast of Alaska to pull up massive scoops of the ocean floor. They would then wash and screen through this incredible amount of muck, mud, and rock to look for gold. Often, they had to go through *massive* amounts of this junk, many tons of it, to find any gold at all. But the thing about it is, as I write this, the price of gold is very high—on the order of $1,600 per troy ounce. So even a few nuggets could make all that work worth the effort.

The same is true with business; in fact, that's what hunting

59

for prospects is all about. **Now, again, even though you do have to go through a lot of unprofitable leads to find the few good ones, that doesn't mean the poorer prospects aren't worth anything.** They're just not potential customers, at least for that particular marketing campaign. So you have to eliminate these folks in some way in order to maximize your efforts—ideally, by making them select themselves out of the marketing pool.

This doesn't have to be difficult. If you run an ad in a magazine or on TV, the bad prospects just won't respond in the first place. If you send them a postcard touting your new product, they'll just discard it. **The process is painless; you don't have to hear them say no or have them slam the door in your face.** They're putting themselves out of the running automatically, which helps you sort through the huge universe of possibilities until you've trimmed it down to a number that you can handle and focus on.

Think of the whole process as something like receiving a dump truck load of sand with a few gold nuggets in it. Your job is to get, say, one load delivered to your backyard on Saturday; then you and your crew spend the rest of the week shoveling and screening, hunting for the gold. By the end of the week you run out of sand, so another dump truck pulls up with a new load of sand and dumps it—and you get back to work. That's a decent visual representation for what happens when you've got a regular, ongoing new customer acquisition campaign that brings in "X" number of leads each week.

At the end of the week, after you've done your work, you have a collection of pretty rocks, some of which may be pyrite or quartz rather than gold. Now, all these folks have at least some worth; to extend the analogy a little, at the very least you can make some good jewelry out of some of those rocks. Maybe others aren't quite as valuable, but they still look nice, and you can put them in the bottom of a fish tank or use them in your flowerbed. They're not quite gold—that is, not the preferred customers you're looking for. **But those people are in the pile, so you need to refine it a bit more.** One way to do so is to invite the "pretty rocks" group to purchase another product that costs somewhat more than the offer you started with.

Just keep marketing and testing, sifting and sorting until you do find that small pool of best customers. Some end up on your preferred customer list, and stay there because they spend a certain dollar amount with you, or respond to certain offers that prove, in your eyes, that they're qualified to be considered a best customer. Those are your gold nuggets, and you only get one or two out of every few hundred pretty rocks— at best. Those preferred customers will become the core of your business. **They tend to respond best when you make offers, or visit your store the most often, participating almost every time you have a special promotion.**

As for the rest of the pretty stones: don't throw them out. **There's still value there, because they respond occasionally and earn you a little money.** They're not going to be your best customers, but they *are* the next tier down.

Everyone else is raw ore or mud from your marketing perspective. Every once in a while, you may be able to get one of them to respond to something; but you're probably never going to make big profits off them. **Still, like it or not, you've got to draw them into your funnel in order to find the good**

and preferred customers, because you usually can't just look at a name and decide that person represents your profit margin. You never know who it's going to be.

The only way you can really find more gold or diamonds is to go through a bigger pile of rocks and dirt. Oh, you might choose to be more scientific about it by studying geology and geography and picking the most likely locations for gold deposits, but no matter what, you've got to shift many tons of soil in order to profit. **It's just the same in business, except you exchange the geosciences for psychology and demographics.** While all the dull rocks of those poor leads may be worth something to someone's business—that is, they may be ore for something besides gold or diamonds— they're just not worth much to your business.

Once you've filtered out everything you can, push the junk aside and grab another pile of raw material. **You continuously have to sort and organize and shuffle and dig again.** You don't know who's going to be a good customer until they *become* a good customer—although ideally, over time, it'll become easier to spot those who will never be good customers to begin with.

Just be sure to keep on bringing in new people, so you can consistently replenish your pool of best customers. The marketplace is fluid, in that there are always people entering and exiting it. Someone who is a good customer today, who has been a good customer for months or years, may stop being a good customer tomorrow. They may move or die, or they might just leave your market for some reason you can't predict. **So in a sense, there's a hole in the bottom of your bucket; if you**

don't work to keep that bucket filled, you'll lose revenue as people fall out. That's the only way to do it, because you can't avoid having that hole there, and you can't fix it short of holding people at gunpoint (literally or figuratively) and forcing them to be your customers.

Never stop looking for that next batch of leads. As long as you have enough leads coming in, and you've got a process in place for filtering out the gold nuggets within that ton of leads, then you're always going to be in business if you've built in decent profit margins. **This is as close to a sure thing as you're going to find in the business world. Keep at it, and you'll never have to worry about having enough money ever again.**

CHAPTER FIVE

Most marketers are weak.

◆ They quit way too soon.

◆ They are too worried about offending their prospects or customers.

◆ Or, they simply don't know that there is a great deal more money laying on the table that could and should be theirs — if they simply went after it more aggressively and then stayed after it until they got it!

Most Marketers Are Weak

Let's face it: most marketers are weak. This isn't intended as a judgment; it's just an observation. **They tend to be weak for three interrelated reasons: 1) They quit way too soon; 2) they're worried about offending their prospects or customers; and 3) they don't realize that there's a lot more money on the table that could be theirs if they just went after it more aggressively.** While there are probably other things that some marketers are doing to create this sense of weakness, these are the big, obvious characteristics that most share. **This is really good news for you, though, because all you have to do is become strong in the areas they're weak in, and you'll have a huge advantage in the marketplace.**

Now, nobody starts out being a great marketer. **It's a learning process.** Here at M.O.R.E., Inc., we've had to learn how to overcome all three of these problems — and even after more than twenty years, we're still learning. We don't have it all figured out. I'm convinced that anybody who tells you that they *do* have it all figured out is either wrong, or deliberately trying to mislead you. **You should always try to improve, and you *can* always improve.**

In the following pages, I'll provide a few stories about how we corrected these mistakes ourselves, so that hopefully, you can learn from our example.

Let's start with the first issue: the willingness to quit too soon. Back in the early 1990s, we produced a lead generation infomercial in an attempt to sell a rather expensive business opportunity. We offered a free VHS tape, in which we made our offer, to anyone who watched our 30-minute infomercial and liked what they saw. We tested the infomercial in 14 or 15 cities. **It produced a lot of great leads for us, and yet we weren't able to convert enough of those leads to sales to cover the cost of the infomercial itself.**

We met with the producer a couple months afterwards and told him that it didn't work. He kept pressing us about it, asking us what we were doing. **Basically, he kept telling us over and over: "You're giving up on them too soon."** He pointed out that the people who requested the VHS tape and our informational literature were very serious; and yes, the money was an objection that they had, but they needed time to think it through. In the meantime, we needed to keep the pressure on.

It really upset me at the time, because I thought we were doing everything we could to convert those sales. I was coming up with a whole lot of reasons why people weren't buying; but in the end, they were just excuses, because the producer was right. **We *were* giving up on them too soon. You know, just because someone says no 10 times doesn't mean that they're going to say no the 11th time.** Ultimately, good salesmanship is about staying on top of your prospective buyers, keeping that pressure on. We learned that lesson well; so today, when we're convinced that we've got a qualified lead, we do lots of follow-up marketing.

And again, there are things you can do with your marketing

to ensure that you're generating the most qualified prospective buyers in the first place. **For example, you can charge more money for your initial low-cost item.** In any case, once you've acquired those high-quality prospects, you should do all the follow-up marketing you possibly can. **Some of our marketing sequences include as many as 20 different mail pieces, followed by phone calls from sales reps.** We're keeping that pressure on. It's sort of like that Chinese water torture—the little drip of water on the forehead that just never stops. By itself, one drop won't do anything; but cumulatively, they have a lot of impact. That's the way your follow-ups should work. Individually, they may not cause the lead to convert to a sale; but they may do so if you stay after them. So once somebody raises their hand and expresses an interest, keep following up with them.

We had a very successful seminar recently, and one of the reasons it was so successful was that in the months leading up to the event, we followed up extensively with our potential attendees. **We made them a great offer—nothing will replace that—then sent them a follow-up every single day for 12 business days in a row,** reminding them all of the benefits they would get if they attended. We do this all the time with our seminars.

Every year since the mid-1990s, we've done an end-of-the-year promotion. The deadline is December 31. Since everybody is thinking about New Year's Eve, it's a date that really sticks in people's brains. **We tell them that when the clock strikes midnight on December 31, the offer is off the table.** But is it really? No—because no matter how much follow-up marketing we do in December, we always go back to those prospects later. We always extend it to January, constantly following up.

Why? Because situations change. Maybe they got a bonus at work last week, or they inherited some money, or they simply finally decided to take the plunge. So as long as someone is qualified to begin with, you've got to stay on them and keep that pressure on. Just because they say no a number of times doesn't mean they're *always* going to say no. **Remember, good salesmanship is all about keeping the prospects under pressure.**

Here's a personal example: when my stepson Chris got married a few years back, he told me he wanted me to wear a tuxedo to his wedding. Well, I hate tuxedos, so I told him, "No way, dude! You want to see me in a tuxedo? Wait till I die. Then you can have the mortician dress me up however you like. I'm not going to wear a tuxedo while I'm still alive." And, of course, by that point he had known me for long enough to know that it was senseless to argue with me.

But he gave me a lot of lead-time, and he just kept that pressure on, coming at me from different angles, too, because that's part of the art of persuasion. **You don't just repeat the same old things; you mix it up a little.** And just like that Chinese water torture treatment, he kept wearing me down and wearing me down until I finally relented. I *did* wear a tuxedo to his wedding— and I hope he only has one wedding, because I never want to wear a tux again!

Good salesmanship requires a relentless attitude. A strong marketer doesn't assume that a no from a prospect means no forever. As Chris Lakey likes to point out, that marketer assumes that what they're really saying is, "I don't *know* enough yet. Tell me more!"

Now, let's look at the second big mistake: the fact that most marketers are weak because they're too worried about upsetting their prospects. They're never aggressive enough. I know all about that because that used to be my story. It's in my core nature to be something of a people-pleaser... but the older I get, the more I overcome that problem.

Back in the 1990s, we had a test promotion in which we asked people to buy a little package for $20-$30 to prove they were serious. Well, some of them were very upset when they got their packages, because they felt they didn't get their money's worth; we had a lot of complaints along the lines of, "I can't believe I paid $20 and all I got was this!" **And yet, our conversion percentage on the upsell was very good.** Nowadays I look back and believe that if we had just rolled that campaign out fully, we could have made hundreds of thousands or millions of dollars. **But because we had such a large group of people who were complaining, I let that promotion go, despite the high upsell conversion rate—and I've always regretted it.** I was so worried about those non-buyers—the people who were probably never going to buy the upsell anyway—that I took my eyes off the ball. I let the complaints blind me to the potential profits. I'll never do that again.

We're working on a similar promotion going on as I write this. Chris and I call it our "Free Money System." It too starts with a small offer where we ask for $20-30 on the front-end. I fully expect that we're going to have a vocal percentage of prospects who don't take the upsell, because the fulfillment for the front-end offer mostly consists of materials that try to make that upsell; so they're going to be upset. We're taking some precautions here, of course, but not a whole lot. **Our main focus is the percentage of leads who do convert to that upsell.** If it's high again this time, and yet we once again have a lot of people who are upset with what they got for their money... **well, we'll just give refunds to the people who complain and move forward with the campaign.** We've got a very liberal refund policy. We never play games with our customers; if somebody wants their money back, we'll gladly return it.

As long as the conversions are strong on the back-end, then we simply don't care how many refunds we make to the unhappy prospects. What matters the most here is who buys the upsell, not who's upset by the front end. That's something you should keep in mind; in fact, it's a good quote to print out and hang on your wall. **"It doesn't matter who you upset, it just matters who you sell."**

Back when I used to be really worried about what people would think of my products and services, I was in such a position of weakness. Here's one example. We've been having seminars now for over 20 years. During those first 10 years, I was nearly paralyzed with worry that some customer might be upset by something. Nowadays, I don't worry so much. Don't get me wrong: I'm out to serve my customers, and I'll do everything possible to serve them in the highest way I know how. **If they're not happy, we'll make every effort to change that.** But I don't internalize it anymore. I don't let it upset me when people complain.

The ironic thing is, I honestly think I do a better job of serving the customers now that I have that attitude in place. By staying focused on the main goal—i.e., by trying to perform at my highest level for the largest possible number of people—I achieve more success. That's where my heart is every time we do a seminar. **As long as I do my best, I don't worry about not hitting the right chord with every single person.** If somebody's not happy, sure, we'll try to make it right. **But at the same time, a certain freedom comes from staying detached from the outcome.**

The third mistake most marketers make is leaving money on the table that could and should be theirs. Most don't stop to think deeply about the fact that their customers might potentially buy a lot more stuff from them. **They never really realize the insatiability of a good customer—the fact that such a customer wants more and more of what they bought the first time.** Now, the funny thing here is that those customers want something a little different at the same time— which means that you have to give them something that's basically familiar at the core, with some unique overlay.

If this seems a little hard to understand, then my best advice is to look at very successful companies, and see how they're doing it, because they've taken this secret to heart. They understand that customers tend to buy within a certain range. **They're looking for the same basic benefits; but you've got to keep mixing it up at the same time, making things look and feel at least a little different.** So while we have all different kinds of promotions here at M.O.R.E., Inc., we basically just keep running the same successful promotions over and over, while making them look and feel a little bit different.

Here's an example of how we do this. Chris and I are involved in a pet boutique business that we're planning to sell as a kind of franchise across the country (we're still in the development phase). **One of the ways we're making sure we don't leave money on the table is by constantly staying in touch with our customers, offering them more and more great stuff.** We host events two or three times a month, and those events are all pretty much identical—but they're a great way for us to stay in touch with our customer base.

By hosting these events, we're giving our customers the appearance of something new all the time. This month we've got this offer, and next month we've got that one... but the structure of the events is unchanged from one to the next. That same-but-different factor may seem like a bit of a riddle at first; but once you're aware of it, once you look and see how other successful companies are doing it, you'll see that you can do the same thing. **People will always buy a lot more than you think they will, so give them the chance to do so.**

And remember, just because somebody says no nine times doesn't mean they won't say yes on the tenth try. **So don't give up! Stay on top of your prospects.** Don't worry about offending them; focus on trying to give it all you've got! Try to perform at your highest level, and be concerned more about the people you sell than the ones you upset. Whether people are upset with you or not is largely outside of your control.

Keep pushing as long and as hard as you can. Now, I sometimes compare salesmanship to the dating world; but I think you need to remember, too, that marketing is *not* dating. In a dating relationship, no actually means no. That's something we're all familiar with, and most of us play within those guidelines. If we try to go somewhere with a date and that person doesn't want to go there, we respect those bounds and back off. We might try again later, but we'll do something else in the meantime.

We all understand that in the confines of a dating relationship, but you shouldn't assume that a marketing relationship is exactly the same animal. As I've mentioned, as regard to marketing, Chris Lakey likes to say, **"No usually doesn't mean no (N-O). What they're really saying is K-N-O-W... that they don't know enough to say yes."** You haven't convinced them it's worth their time or money to do business with you, so your job as a salesperson is to convince them to say yes.

You can't convince them to say yes unless you keep asking, going at it with different angles under constant contact with a prospect, so that you can discover which angle works for them. This concept will eventually work itself out or wear itself out. **The only time you should listen to them saying no is the point at which it becomes unprofitable to keep trying to get them to say yes.**

To recognize that point, you have to fully understand your marketing model and your expenses—the full costs of doing business and trying to attract more customers. At some point, you'll find that you can't profitably convert more leads to sales. **It may take many steps to get there, but eventually your profits will be less than your costs of new customer**

acquisition. If, say, it costs you $1,000 to follow up with a group of prospects and you netted only $300 in new business, that's when you move on to something else.

Now, the caveat here is that if your model is set up properly, **you can actually lose money on your first sale and still profit in the long run.** In fact, that's going to happen more often than not; but if you keep the lifetime value of your customer in mind, and you have an excellent back-end to help you sell to that customer repeatedly for the maximum possible profit, then it's okay to lose a little money on the first sale. **Overall, you'll make plenty on the additional sales you make to them; so you do have to know and remember those numbers.**

Sadly, many marketers don't keep this in mind. They don't make their costs back immediately, so they give up. **Sometimes it takes 10 to 12 follow-ups — or more — to actually get to the point where you're losing money long-term, and most people give up after one or two tries.** In fact, many give up if they don't make a sale the *first* time they invite a customer to do business with them. So if you're doing any follow-up at all, then you're ahead of the game; but you're still probably not doing enough.

Why don't most marketers try harder? **Their failure is rooted in their fear of offending their clients or prospects.** They're not aggressive enough to get that business that they are, in effect, leaving on the table. It would be theirs if they'd go after it hard enough.

And sure, you *can* offend some prospects. They may tell you during a sales call that they never want you to contact them again, or send you something by mail that basically says the same thing. **Legally, you must honor that request and immediately take them off your call or mailing list. But people who do this are fairly rare.** As long as you're doing a good job marketing in the first place, you won't have to worry much about offending people; because remember, the first goal of your marketing experience is to qualify your customer base and attract the right kind of people, those who are going to be interested in doing business with you long-term. If you do that, and keep providing the kinds of products, information, and services they're interested in, very few will utterly refuse you— unless you do something to *really* make them angry.

Even when people ask to be removed from your list, you'll often find that they're rejecting you because the original prospect has moved without informing you of their new address, or they're deceased, or some other scenario has come about where the person you're trying to reach is no longer there. If you've done your homework, mismatches like this are rare; so you don't have to worry too much about people asking you to stop communicating with them. In that case, why should you ever stop?

If you're like most marketers, communication stops because you've given up on the person too soon. That's your fault, not theirs. At some point, they qualified themselves, or they wouldn't be on your list. **If they've requested information from you, then they want to hear what you have to say. So, you have to ramp up the aggressiveness and stay on top of them.** We call this "ruthless marketing." It's not ruthless in the nasty sense; it's just a strategy for aggressively trying to attract all the business you can. You refuse to give up on your customers until they've proven that it's not profitable to keep trying to do business with them. That might mean that your model consists of half a dozen follow-ups, or 10, 12, or 15.

We've had follow-up sequences of more than 20 mailings. **We continued to follow up because the model was right, and because it was a high-profit item**—we could afford to send a lot of mail to invite them to do business with us. In other cases, we've found that about half a dozen follow-ups are ideal to attract the right number of customers; after that, it becomes unprofitable to continue.

Just don't worry about offending people who aren't your intended prospects. Now, some people are timid marketers in the sense that they want to be politically correct; they want to do anything they can to avoid any sign of rudeness, any potential offense, even language that might be distasteful or seem too aggressive to somebody. They go out of their way to be as polite and nice as possible. And yes, there are times to be polite; but don't let the desire to be that way get in the way of making a profit. **You don't have to be rude to aggressively promote your product or service, but you do need to be persistent.**

Realize that sometimes, that persistence can rub people the wrong way. Accept it and move on. So what if some people find you annoying? **If you're reaching and attracting the right kinds of prospects, you'll find that your sales will increase as a result of your persistence.** You just have to keep your eyes on the numbers. And do be aware that depending on your model, price structure, profit margin, and expenses, this kind of marketing can have horrible numbers (in terms of percentage rates) and still be extremely profitable. Let's say you totally offend half of your prospects; that's still 50 out of 100 people who *aren't* going to be offended. Out of those 50, you might get three orders. **That's a 3% success rate, which isn't unusual.** Well, if you've set it all up right, you can still make plenty of money. Plus, the 47 prospects you didn't offend are still possibilities. Your first message just didn't hit them at the right time, for some reason.

Ultimately, you're not going to sell everybody on your product or service; in fact, only a handful are going to become customers. **You have to go through a lot of noes to get to the yeses.** Those are the ones you care about and focus on; if you worry about pleasing everyone, you'll find it hard to please anyone.

The things you do to get the right people to say yes are inherently going to make other people say no. Your price may be the deciding factor; if you have a premium priced product, of course you're pricing a lot of people out of your marketplace. If you sell something for $3,000-5,000, only people that have that kind of cash on hand are going to be doing business with you. Other people might call or write and say, "I can't afford this! Why don't you make something more affordable for me?" Well, maybe you don't *want* to make something more affordable. Maybe you have your reasons for the price.

Again: whatever your model is, you have to worry about who you're attracting, not about who you're offending. You don't have to be rude or brash about it, although I've seen marketers use that MO effectively. The point is, **you're going to offend some people no matter what, simply as a consequence**

of attracting the right kinds of people and aggressively going after them. Accept that.

If you offer an easy out for prospects, then you should be completely unafraid of offending them, particularly in the process of lead generation. As I've mentioned, we often require someone to spend a little money to become our prospect, via a small qualifying purchase. Sometimes that's as little as $9; it may be a little more, like $19 or $29 or $39. In many cases, what they mostly get for that purchase is an invitation to do further business with us by buying one of our more expensive packages. And yes, some people do get upset with that. **Well, the reason that we make that model work is because we give them an easy out.** We tell them through our Guarantee Policy that if they're not happy with the material they receive, they just have to let us know. We give them a toll-free cancellation number they can call 24/7; **we'll refund their money, and they don't even have to send anything back. That takes the pressure, stress, and worry off them.**

This helps us, too, by taking them out of the marketing pool. We're not trying to rip people off just so we can make a few bucks short-term. **We're looking for people who will buy more products and services from us in the future.** The process works pretty well, too; a decent number of the prospects we send our front-end materials to are happy to step up to the next level. Some we never hear from again. But if someone calls us and they're upset about what they've gotten, then we can easily point to that refund policy and give them their money back.

We're not getting rich on those front-end prices. **We're just trying to do two things: help offset the cost of the mailing,**

and attract a qualified prospect. When someone is upset, it's easy to defuse that by giving them their money back, so they can go about their day—and so we can go find the people who will say yes. That's why we always encourage you to have very liberal refund policies: so you can aggressively attract as many yeses as possible without the fear of offending the noes.

Keep your eyes open, and you'll see how most marketers are doing a terrible job in all three of the areas I've covered in this here. They don't stay in touch with their prospective buyers, they're not doing any kind of aggressive follow-up marketing, they're not trying to sell their prospects additional products and services, and their marketing message is too homogenized. They're trying to be so perfect that they really have no personality at all. Admittedly, they're not offending anybody—but they're really not *attracting* anybody either.

So think about how you can do the exact opposite, becoming strong in all the areas they're weak in—and gain tremendous confidence knowing that you can get out there and dominate your market!

CHAPTER SIX

"The most important thing in life
is not to capitalize on your gains.
Any fool can do that! The really important
thing is to profit from your losses.
That requires intelligence and it
makes the difference between
a wise man and a fool."

William Boltho, Twelve Against the Gods

Profit from Your Losses

In his book *12 Against the Gods*, William Boltho has this to say: "The important thing in life is not to capitalize on your gains. Any fool can do that! **The really important thing is to profit from your losses. That requires intelligence, and it makes the difference between a wise man and a fool.**"

This particularly applies to business—where, frankly, more things are going to go wrong than go right. You have to realize that from the beginning. Get your arms around it; embrace it. Business can be the ultimate heartbreaker, so here's a very simple three-step strategy you can use to profit from your losses. Use these steps again and again; make them a way of life, and a way of business.

I've already mentioned the first step: **Expect problems. Accept them as an ongoing and necessary part of life.** Since business is life accelerated, you'll encounter problems daily; so face them head on. Typically, to get ahead you have to run *towards* what other people are running away *from*. While there are some problems that you should try to avoid, there *are* good things about problems in general. **So try to re-train your brain to realize that problems are mostly issues looking for a solution: solutions that equal wealth, especially if you can solve something once and for all.**

Another good thing about problems is they spur you

into action. Because problems don't feel good, the pressure forces you to get to work on fixing them. **All business should be about action and movement and solutions that will get you and your customers out of painful situations.** The pain will always be there to some degree; you can't stop that. **But you** *can* **redirect that pain into constructive energy.**

The first step in doing so is to refocus on how you think about problems, realizing that they're good and that they're necessary—that you just have to suck it up, step up, and move through them. Don't just expect everything to work out all by itself. Part of what drives people crazy in business is that they're looking for a panacea, a perfect world. They think that if they go into business, then everything is going to be great. "I got rid of my boss—now I'm self-employed!" Well, the newly self-employed don't want to hear it, but that just results in you having to handle a lot more problems personally. That's reality, you see: being in business means *more* problems, not fewer. There's only one way to avoid any problems at all, and that's to die.

The second step here is to look for the good within the bad. Recall that old saying: it's an ill wind that blows no good. So while you're suffering through the pain, try to find at least one silver lining to hold onto... and find it as fast as you can. Think back to some of the more difficult problems that you've faced in the past. Ultimately, some good probably came out of those situations. At the time you were overwhelmed, and maybe you couldn't see an out; you might have felt hopeless, as if you couldn't handle it. **And yet, you made it through and moved forward, often with some new solution or lesson in hand.**

Most of us have experienced this type of situation.

The trick here is to shorten the time you're mired in the problem. So ask yourself: "What's good about this situation?" At first the answer will probably be, "Nothing! Nothing at all is good about this." But keep asking yourself: "Well, what *could* be good about it?", and try to maintain both your perspective and your sense of humor along the way. **Step back and realize that what you're going through now probably won't matter at all in 10 years, or possibly five—or maybe even in five days.** Try to find something funny about the situation, to take the sting out and relax a little.

Third, take massive action in finding a solution to that pressure and pain. That will allow you to re-channel your energy into fixing the problem. Just go crazy with the ideas, coming up with as many possibilities as you can. **You may not know which is going to work, but at least you're moving toward fixing the problem instead of running away and hiding.** Even better, you're constructively using energy that many people use destructively when they encounter problems. So get moving.

While you're doing all this, move forward with the determination that you're not going to just keep having the same problems over and over again. Problems may be good for you at one level, but bouncing off the same ones repeatedly isn't. **The idea is to grow and learn from your mistakes—to try to get better, so that your old problems are no longer problems at all.** That's one edge you have when you stay with one marketplace for a long time. When you've developed loads of knowledge and experience and confidence because you've solved a lot of problems along the way, you have a tremendous competitive advantage over all of the people who are just getting started. They're still going to have to go through all the same crap you already did, discovering their own solutions as they do so.

You can usually tell when you encounter someone who has fought through to the point where they've learned how to solve all the common problems in their field. They express a quiet but very real confidence. It's not a loud thing; it doesn't have to be. They just don't have to worry about those things that are freaking other people out and driving them crazy, because they've been there and gone through it all. **They've integrated the solutions into their skill-set, and they have a competitive edge.**

We've got an annual event we call our Wealth Explosion Seminar. This year, 2012, represents our fourth annual event. **In the past, I've sweated bullets while preparing for live seminars like these.** Quite often, what happens when you promote these events is that two-thirds of the people sign up in the last third of the promotion process. So if you're promoting over a nine-month period, then **most of the people are going to commit only in the last two and a half or three months.** This means that although you may be pushing the seminar hard, you don't get a lot of results right away—which may then worry you. That's certainly how I respond. I'm constantly worried, because we have these fixed costs of the hotel and the rent for that big lecture room. Then I get scared that nobody's going to show up, and I'll end up with about seven people in the audience.

These are things that I've had to go through every year.

We're committed to doing this annual event; we love to do it. It's good for us, it's good for the business, it's good for our staff, it's good for our relationship with our joint venture partners, and it's good for all the customers—even those who never come to the event, because at least they know we've got nothing to hide. **We're constantly reaching out to them and trying to get them to attend, showing them that we're trustworthy and honest.**

But it's so difficult! Ever since 9-11, it's gotten harder and harder to do seminars. People don't want to travel as much, so getting them to do so is painful. Well, that pain has become too great, and I recently decided I couldn't go through it again; so I decided that this next year, we're going to try something different. **We went into massive action mode, letting the pain of those old problems spur us into action. We put our energy into a new solution, and it's working phenomenally well right now.** We expect to have an awesome event this time, without some of the pressures that I've had to worry about in previous years. If it works as I expect it to, we're going to keep doing it every year…until it doesn't work anymore. When new problems present themselves and become overwhelming, we'll just go into massive action mode again.

We've had plenty of experience doing things like this, because we've had plenty of problems over the years. Business really can be quite painful. But never forget that there's one basic, golden solution to almost every single problem you'll ever encounter in business: just make more sales and profits. **Sell your way out of those problems by selling more stuff to more people, more often, for more profit per transaction.** You'll find that most of your problems occur because you don't have enough money: you can't pay your bills, you can't pay your taxes, you can't pay your employees, or you can't pay yourself. Injecting more money will solve all those problems, so focus on your sales so you can channel the pain of the financial struggle into that positive area.

Chris Lakey was telling me recently about an episode of the TV show "Gold Rush" on the Discovery Channel, which documents the efforts of modern gold miners in Alaska. I mentioned it in an earlier. Well, in this episode, they were following one mine where this 17-year-old kid has taken over. His grandfather is the owner of the operation, but he's getting up there in age. He still helps out a little bit, while the kid's running the place over the summer before school starts. There's a lot of stress happening in this mine, and as they're dialoging back and forth they're talking how the stress levels are all elevated because it's been a down year so far and they need so much gold each week just to break even—to pay for all their equipment and the workers. It's wild to watch this all take place, because they're looking for what ends up being just a few ounces of gold in a huge mass of dirt. It amounts to a tiny jarful in truckloads of soil.

In the episode Chris watched, they'd found five or six thousand dollars worth that week, and that was going to be just about enough to pay for the costs of operation. This 17-year-old kid was talking about his past experience, when they were finding lots of gold. Things were going well; they were making plenty of money, and everybody was getting paid on time. But at the time of that particular episode, that wasn't the case. **They were**

struggling, so emotions were high. There was a lot of tension, a lot of stress, and that made them say things they wished they hadn't said and make decisions based on their immediate needs, instead of what was in their real long-term interest.

When things go bad and you're dealing with adversity, that's the time to step up your game and find a way to profit from those situations. Now, realize that profiting may not mean immediately making money. It may just mean learning from the experience and arranging things so you'll do better next time.

There are few completely negative experiences; you can learn something from just about every outcome, though obviously there are wins and losses. I'm not one of those people who claims that every experience isn't really a positive or a negative, that it all just evens out; that's not reality, and most people can't really process things that way. **But I do think you can learn new ways to grow and prosper from all your experiences, if you can just get past the outcomes.** That's your choice: either learn and grow, or suffer through those ordeals with no real benefit.

And remember, treat it as a game. In life, you need to play to win; but sometimes, like it or not, you either just break even or come out behind in some of the individual games of a particular "season." **That's fine, because your ultimate goal is what matters, not the individual skirmishes.** Consider an NFL football team: the goal is to win the Super Bowl. Even though a team may experience loss along the way, that doesn't sidestep the players from their ultimate goal of being the ones to hold up that Lombardi trophy in celebration at the end of the season. That's the long-term prize that the serious player keeps shooting for all year, whether he's practicing, taking part in pre-season games, or working his way through the regular season.

Here in Goessel, we root for the Kansas City Chiefs. The last coach they had before the current one always said that his strategy was to look at the season as four four-game bites. His goal was to achieve at least a 3-1 record in a particular "bite." Now, he never wanted that one loss, but to be realistic, there are times you can't win; so he treated each quarter as its own little micro-season, and tried to string those winning quarters together to make the playoffs. At that point, they could determine how to work through the playoffs on the way toward winning the Super Bowl.

Apply that attitude to your business. **The ultimate goal is to win the big prize at the end.** How you play the game throughout the season, and how you adjust and react to your experiences, will determine whether you meet that goal or fall short in some way. Don't assume that a specific loss is the end for you; accept the situation, try to learn from it, and apply that knowledge to the next "game."

In my experience, you experience the most growth while adapting to difficult times, and you end up much tougher than you might have been. I believe that people who don't suffer through any adversity—whether they're born with silver spoons in their mouths, or just have incredible luck—are usually the ones who suffer the most in the end. They have no idea how to respond to a negative situation when one occurs; and so they end up crushed, because they've never had to learn how to take care of themselves or how to handle a challenge. You may view them with envy while they're experiencing their good times, but they're the ones who really do suffer in the end.

Conversely, the people who are able to push through a hard life, to keep on going through pain and trauma to shine in the end, are the ones that we really admire. Those are the people they do the TV specials and make movies about. Their ability to overcome adversity makes them inspirational; and ultimately, they've become better people as a result of those challenges. No one likes to go through negative experiences, but in the end, they often refine us, making us better people. **That's what you should shoot for: to learn from those adversities, to find ways to profit in the losses.** If you can learn to profit during the bad times, you'll be much better prepared to profit during the *good* times.

Many of us see the great, shining examples of business success, like Bill Gates and Ted Turner, and forget that those people had to fight their way to the top. **In fact, until you read their biographies, you never understand about the mountains of failure they had to overcome to get there.** What you see is somebody with a lot of skill, a lot of ability, a lot of confidence, and usually a lot of wealth... and you tend to envy those people without realizing all they had to go through to get there.

And remember: the people we admire the most are also the ones who typically exhibit the most *real* confidence. I'm not talking about some ego trip, where they're running around thinking they're better than everybody else. That's egotism, not real confidence; and it's usually a defense mechanism. **The people we admire the most are the honestly confident, and that confidence doesn't develop overnight.** It's not something

93

you can just turn off and on or use as a façade.

Here's a quote from the 16th century that I think exemplifies this fact: "Confidence is a plant of slow growth." It takes time and effort to work through all the problems you face, and develop those skills that lead to real confidence. **So learn the lessons that loss teaches you, accept them into your heart, and keep moving forward.**

CHAPTER SEVEN

❄ ❄ ❄

Take away selling:

Sometimes when you say "No!" — it only makes them want you more!

❄ ❄ ❄

Sometimes When You Say "No," It Only Makes Them Want You More

Making something scarce, and then telling people they can't have it, is a good way to stoke the fire of their desire. Now, this is a pretty simple idea, and it applies to other aspects of life besides business. Consider the world of dating, where people talk about playing hard to get; basically, this means you let the other person do the chasing. You always hold back a little, and essentially you run until the other person catches you. This also works in business negotiations, which is what every transaction tends to boil down to. After all, you're asking someone to give you their money in exchange for whatever it is you're offering them; that's the very definition of negotiation.

Well, in every negotiation, whoever wants it the least— or at least pretends they do—wields the most power. Now, when both parties in a deal realize this and both are trying to play that game, the results can be amusing... because nothing gets done, as people pretend they just don't care what happens. That's not a good business move in general, but to some extent, there's always a little game-playing going back and forth in a business transaction. One person has more power than the other person—with power being defined as the ability to act.

You need to make sure you're that person as often as you possibly can.

One of the ways to do this is to always be willing to say

no. Establish that early on in the negotiation, because in many cases, it makes people want whatever you have even more. **It's just human nature for people to desire rare things that they have a hard time getting.** That being the case, you have to put up barriers to entry—even if they're fake sometimes. **Arrange things so people have to work to cross those barriers, and they'll want what you have to offer at least a little more.**

If that seems like manipulation to you, well, I say it's only manipulative if what you're selling is total crap that doesn't deliver on your promises. If, on the other hand, you've got something really valuable that really *can* deliver (or over-deliver) on the promises you're making, then you should use this strategy as fully as possible. **If you're serving people by helping them get what they want, then it's not manipulative to sell to them as hard as you can.** As long as you're genuine, you're just making them see that they need what you have, and stoking their interest a bit.

Another reason this principle works is that, quite simply, desperation and neediness is not an attractor factor. What *is* attractive? Typically, people who don't scramble to get what they're after. They often seem not to care that much one way or another. Conversely, you often want to just run from desperate, needy people. They make you uncomfortable and you don't want to deal with them. There's something inside of us that perceives desperation as a warning.

That's why it's a good idea to run until the prospect catches you. Not only do you want to let people feel that what you have is exclusive—something they should be grateful that they got involved with at all, and that you *let* them get involved with—you should never be too eager about it. You have to hold back... or at least appear to. We call this takeaway selling.

Recently, I arranged the first steps of a business deal that could be huge for M.O.R.E., Inc., if I can work it out—and the truth is, I want it bad. **But I set the stage for it very carefully.** First, I had a third party set up a call to the person I wanted to deal directly with. I already knew that person, but I hadn't seen or spoken to her in about 15 years; so it wasn't as if I could just pick up the phone and call her. **But she was waiting for my phone call, because somebody who's very close to her set that call up for me.**

During the phone call, I underplayed the whole deal. I made what I thought was a very attractive offer, given what I know about this potential joint venture partner, but I didn't apply any pressure aside from letting her know what I knew. I just put it out there that I was interested, never making it appear that I was desperate for the deal to go through. **I was nonchalant about the whole thing. I did that deliberately, because if you come on too fast and too strong, people will just run away.**

Holding back is integral to the concept of takeaway selling. The more you hold back, the more you let them run after you rather than you running after them. **And remember: in business, the chaser is in a weaker position than the one being chased.**

Apart from the dislike of desperation, this is all about scarcity and exclusivity. **Exclusivity inflames people's greed a little.** When you purposely keep the numbers down, people see something and feel it's very special—and they want it. Here's a good example: we're currently promoting a seminar where we limit the attendees to just 100 people and their special guests. **We're telling them that thousands of these invitations are going out, which is true; but we're taking just one hundred positions, on a first come, first served basis.** That's one form of takeaway selling.

The marketing consultant who first taught us this principle told a story that I'll never forget, and I want to pass it on to you. When he was first getting started he was dirt poor, struggling to make ends meet, barely able to pay his bills and keep a roof over his head. **And yet when he got ahold of a really hot prospect, and knew it could lead to a lot more business, he acted a bit reluctant.** The prospect asked him, "Now, what does your schedule look like for next week?" and the marketing consultant said quickly, "Oh, sorry, next week I'm booked solid. Actually, I'm booked solid the week after that, too... But I think I might have an opening in about two and a half weeks. Let me check my calendar." And all this, when he had no work at all!

But if he'd said, "I can come see you right now—I've got plenty of time at the moment," then all of a sudden this hot prospect might not have been so hot anymore. The desperation factor might have sunk the opportunity. The consultant knew that he had to appear to be too busy, because he wanted it to seem that people were so eager to obtain his services that his schedule was packed full. He wanted that prospect to chase him.

Again, assuming you can deliver on your goods, this strategy isn't unfairly manipulative. **When your products or services really do provide the benefits you promise, then it's worthwhile in the end.** In this case, when the marketing consultant got hired by his hot prospect and then produced the results the prospect wanted, that was a win-win situation. A manipulative situation is one in which one party arranges things so they win, but the other party loses: basically, they cheated that person. They didn't deliver on their promises.

And if you tell people up front that the offer is limited, then how can it ever be a manipulative situation? Often, we actually apologize in advance when we have a limited offer. We tell people right there in the sales literature and our promotional presentations, "Look, if all the positions are gone by the time you call, we apologize—and we'll even send you our written apology. Of course we'll send your money back, and we'll even include a free gift." We do little things like that because it drives the point home to people. **If you're selling an exclusive deal, then there really does have to be a cut-off point, or else you'll lose all credibility—and the deal will lose value for those who already have it, because they believed that it was, in fact, exclusive.**

We just sold a limited position in a new opportunity and we told people clearly, "This is going to be limited. There will only be so many people allowed in, and we're going to keep that number small." **Then we actually did it. The truth is, we actually cut off participation much sooner than we had to.** We could have kept selling new positions indefinitely, just like that going-out-of-business store that never goes out of business. **But we wanted to be strictly true to our word.**

So when you do this, again, it's not about cheating or manipulating people. You're telling the truth in a way that makes people feel good about what you're trying to sell them. **And the**

harder that product or service is to obtain, the more they want it; that's human nature. Therefore, the less eager you appear, or the more you hold back and let them chase you, the better. **They're very grateful then when the deal goes through, and there's less buyer's remorse, which often comes back to haunt you in other transactions.** That's another good reason why you should put some barriers in place: it makes the buyer feel good about the purchase.

Takeaway selling works on multi-billion dollar deals, too. I recently read the book *Steve Jobs,* the excellent Walter Isaacson biography about the late founder of Apple Computers, and then listened to the audio book. There's a story in there about how Disney bought Jobs' animation company Pixar; you've seen their movies, like the *Toy Story* series. **They bought it for over seven *billion* dollars.** Well, during the negotiation, the Pixar people wanted it bad, and they were fired up about the prospect.

Steve Jobs went into the final negotiations with a fellow named John Lassiter, who was running the operation over at Pixar. Lassiter is apparently a very enthusiastic person at all times—he's like a little kid that way. As they were riding the elevator up to the Executive Suite, Lassiter could barely contain himself—the offer from Disney was such a once-in-a-lifetime deal. But he knew his excitement was a weakness in the negotiation, so told Steve Jobs, **"Anytime I start getting too excited, kick me underneath the table." And sure enough, Steve did have to kick him underneath the table.**

John Lassiter knew, just as Steve Jobs did, that the more he seemed to want the deal, the weaker his position was. **The more he acted like it was no big deal, the more power he had.**

102

Ultimately, he had $7 billion worth of power.

Think about that.

Takeaway selling is rooted in human psychology, with the old supply-and-demand concept acting as the psychological lever. When there's plenty of something available, demand is usually diminished because there's no scarcity there; you can have it easily enough if you want it. This is as true for gold as it is for goldfish. **If supplies of something are scarce *and* people want it (both those factors have to be in play), then prices go up.** There's more excitement, more of a buzz around it, and many people will be willing to pay just about anything to get it, just because there's not enough to go around.

That's most of the reason why gold is more expensive than pyrite or brass, and why diamonds are more expensive than cubic zirconium. **Now, in these cases the real things do have their special uses; but mostly people just want something that others don't have.** The scarcer it is, the more the demand goes up—and the higher the price you can charge for it.

When you master the art of takeaway selling, you're essentially creating a short-circuited supply chain. You can do this with an actual physical commodity, but it also works very well with information products. Reducing the availability will make people want whatever it is that you have even more.

Chris Lakey is currently into an interesting TV show called *American Pickers*. It's about these folks from Iowa who travel all over the Midwest, mostly, looking for antiques. The name of their business is "Antique Archeology," and they hunt for what they call "rusty gold"—old, rusty, worn-out items no one really notices. Most people would throw them away. They often go to places out in the country where the owner's been collecting junk, auction items, and various such things for decades. They pick through it, looking for items that they can put in their store and on their website to sell.

The reason this comes to mind is because they often get into negotiations for various items, and they'll use takeaway psychology during the negotiations. In the commentary, sometimes they'll admit that they were really eager to buy a particular item and they just had to have it... but they didn't want to show that. Usually, if it seems like just a piece of junk, they can get it for a low price. But occasionally you'll see them slip up and you can tell that they're *really* excited about something—and as a result, so is the seller. Because they're really excited about it, they're willing to pay more for it; and when the seller realizes that, they'll hold out for a higher price. It's the smart thing to do.

On an episode Chris watched recently, they paid $8,000 for two items. One was an old engine, and they weren't sure exactly what it even went to; the other was basically the rusty old frame to a motorcycle, I think. If I'd seen those things, I would have said they were junk, and could probably be tossed out. But they got back to the shop and discovered that those two items were worth at least a few thousand dollars more than they had paid for them. **They probably could have acquired the items for a lower price, but during the negotiation they pretty much let the cat out of the bag that they were really excited about them.** As a result, the gentleman who was selling the items knew how badly they wanted them—that they weren't planning on going home without taking those things with them—and so he raised the price.

Based on this real-life example, it's easy to see that being too eager for something can hurt you, whatever side of the equation you're on. As the buyer, of course, you're in one position; but as the seller, you have to create the feeling that the prospect will miss out on what you're offering if they're unwilling to pay the asking price. **The removal of the item from the table makes them want it more, assuming you've done a good job of matching your marketplace to your offer so you know that people really *are* interested.**

If something is obviously rare, it's easy to do this. **If, on the other hand, you have an apparently endless supply of something, you have to get creative with your takeaway selling.** We often have this problem in information marketing, because many items can be endlessly duplicated on paper, CD, or DVD. There *is* no inherent scarcity. On the other hand, if I were selling an antique, maybe there were only a few thousand of them made in the first place; and in the 75 years since, most have been destroyed or lost, and quite possibly there are only a handful left in existence. That's *real* scarcity, and it just naturally increases the value of that item.

That's not the case with information products, whether they're books or CDs. **If people want more, the supply can be adjusted to meet demand, which makes takeaway selling all the harder.** But let me repeat: the supply *can* be adjusted to meet the demand... which means it can be adjusted downward or otherwise limited to increase the demand, all other things being equal. **You can, and must, create an artificial scarcity in circumstances of abundance.**

I've seen marketers make a big deal about how they've actually destroyed the master copy of something in order to accomplish this. They might have shredded the original paper copy, cut apart the master CD, or smashed the hard drive of the computer it was stored on (though I'm not sure anyone has ever gone that far). **The point is, once the copies they made from that master are gone, they're gone—period. After that, the only way to share to information again is to make a new version of it. That creates an environment of scarcity.**

If there's no master copy because of the type of information product involved, you can still use this principle; for example, with an event-driven sale, where there's a fixed deadline. Just tell them, "If you don't get your reservation in by this date, you'll miss out, because we're only allowing a few people to attend." You might even give them a reason: "The fire marshal says that our conference room can safely hold only 75 people—so if we allowed in 76, we'd get in trouble... and might have to cancel the event altogether. We're not going to let that happen, so if you're the 76th person to try reserve your position, you're out of luck." That limits the availability, and makes people want it more.

As a side note, you can deliberately create such experiences by reserving small conference rooms instead of large ones. At our last big event in Branson, Missouri, we saw a meeting room that easily holds 2,500 people. If we decided to hold an event for everyone who might possibly want to attend, we'd definitely book that place. But for both economic and marketing reasons, there's no sense in us doing that. **It's more effective to talk to smaller groups, and since limiting the attendance helps drive up the interest in the event, then why not limit it?** We can tell our prospects, "The room only holds so many people, so if you want in on the action, you need to act now. We'll soon be sold out. If you miss the boat, we'll have to return your money and tell you better luck next year."

The best way to implement a plan like this is to throw it all out there to them. **Make them really, really want what you have, and then make it where they have to show you that they want it in order to get it—or give them the possibility of missing out on it in some capacity.** If you've got them salivating over what you're offering, to the point where they're just about committed to buying it, then threatening to take it away will be the icing on the cake that makes them *have* to have it.

Going back to *American Pickers*: on another recent show, one of the pickers saw this radio microphone from the 1950s. Now, those old fashion microphones just have a certain look to them; and I'm sure you'll immediately be able to picture one in your head, having seen them before on TV and in the movies. This one was on a stand, and looked like it was used in a studio of some kind, or possibly on a stage somewhere. It was just beautiful, with a nice silvery shine, and appeared to be in great condition. Well, the picker instantly knew that, as a classic item, it had great value to collectors.

When he inquired about it, the owner went into its history a little; and after a while, he told the pickers that he actually had two of them, and wasn't sure he wanted to part with either one.

Well, that created some tension in the picker; he was very interested in the microphone, and was quickly sold on it... and suddenly it looked like he wasn't going to get it, because the owner wasn't sure he wanted to sell. That made the picker want it even more, and ultimately, he spent more money for it than he normally would have—and possibly more than he had to.

This example illustrates the power of takeaway selling. **But for the effect to work, the prospect has to be sold on the item in the first place.** If you're not interested in an item, then who cares how many there are in stock? I can go to Wal-Mart to shop for all kinds of things, and there are still thousands of items available in the store that I know nothing about and I'm not interested in, because I'm not there to buy those items. But if I go there looking for a certain kind of food and they're out of it, I'm upset, because I was already sold on it. It doesn't matter how many other items they happen to have in stock that day; the one thing I wanted was unavailable, and that annoys me as a shopper.

Create the need, and then take it away—or at least threaten to. It heightens the value of the product or service. Ultimately, you can negotiate a "no" to your advantage, and still leave the prospect feeling good about what they bought from you. **You'll almost always get a better result by holding back, or by being willing to walk away from a deal.**

CHAPTER EIGHT

Continuing to make <u>BIG MONEY</u> over a period of years never happens by accident. It is *always* the result of high intention, sincere effort, intelligent direction, and skillful execution. It represents the wise choices of many alternatives and the cumulative experience you gain from all the years of disciplined and focused work.

Big Money is No Accident

Continuing to make big money for long periods of time never happens by accident. **It's always the result of high intention, sincere effort, intelligent direction, and skillful execution.** It represents the wise choice selected from many alternatives, and the application of experience gained from years of disciplined and focused work.

When you get right down to it, getting rich is formulaic. It's kind of like a cake recipe. If it's a good recipe to begin with, you can end up with a nice cake if you follow the directions to the letter—even if you're not a good cook. You add specific ingredients, mix them a specific way, and bake the mix in a specific type of pan at a specified temperature. Follow the procedure point by point, and you're guaranteed good results.

Getting rich, or succeeding in *anything*, is exactly like that.

Let's take a look at **high intention** first. **When I think of high intention, I think of setting big goals. How high is high for you?** What do you really want to accomplish? I'm working on a sales letter right now, and I've just written down a goal for that letter. I want it to be the best performing, most profitable letter I've ever written—period. I wrote that little goal down just so I could motivate and inspire myself; but that's what having high intentions is all about. **You need to set goals that stir your blood, that get you pumped up.**

I try to set simple goals before every project to inspire myself. Sometimes the goal I specify is the amount of money I want to generate, so I'll write down actual numbers—high numbers, so I'll get excited about them and stay focused. Now, goal setting is not an exact science; it's flawed in some ways, and different things work better for different people at different times. But still, having high intentions, always wanting to do your very best and perform at your highest level, is crucial. This also helps you determine how high is high for you. **Continuing to push yourself beyond your limits and biting off more than you can chew, and trying to go for bigger and better things by dint of sincere effort, is what high intention is all about.**

Now, I do believe in working smart—but I also know that you have to work hard at the same time. **One of the things I believe in very strongly is the idea of "pace yourself, but push yourself."** Some people claim that stress is a terrible thing, but it's really strain that's terrible, not stress. Stress is actually okay as long as you pace yourself. Look, if hard work alone made people rich, then millionaires would be much more common than they are. But it's still an important part of the success formula, and **nothing will replace sincere effort.** That's the second element here.

The third is intelligent direction. As I like to say, **you have to see it bigger and think it simpler.** Look at every project in a grand conceptual manner, so you're thinking big, but strip away all the bells and whistles so you've reduced it to its basics—the things that really matter. **If you don't put intelligent direction in play, you're likely to start focusing on all the details and get overwhelmed.** When you get overwhelmed, you're going to lock up—and if that happens, you won't be able to stay in the game long enough to succeed. So before you start, think things through so you can identify what really matters. There's a quote attributed to Abraham Lincoln: "If I had three hours to chop down a tree, I'd spend the first two hours sharpening my ax." That's what intelligent direction is all about.

Skillful execution is one of the areas I struggle with the most. Implementation is not my strong suit. I love dreaming up big ideas, but when it comes to executing those ideas, I often drop the ball. Thank goodness I have a magnificent management team, because in large part, they're the ones who end up carrying through the skillful execution. **I'm like a lot of entrepreneurs: I'm great at dreaming up the big ideas (if I do say so myself), but when it comes to putting it all together and making it all work, I suck!** That's why my wife Eileen was our President and CEO for the first 12 years of our business, until she had to step down for health reasons. Eileen is very analytical, she's very common sense, she focuses on details, and she's very good at implementation. Our current General Manager, Shelly Webster, is a lot like my wife.

So there you have it: the four areas this particular formula focuses on. **That's how you make big money consistently, especially when you apply them to the wise choices of many alternatives.** There are so many different things you can do here, so you have to experiment until you find those few things that will produce the biggest results. After you've been in the same market for a while, you'll intuitively recognize some of those things. That's one of the best benefits of doing something year after year; eventually, the tremendous power of intuition starts to guide you. You may not have all the answers figured out, but you do have a good gut feeling of how to proceed.

To really make the big bucks, you have to have an intuitive feel for what works and what doesn't: what you should move toward, and what you should move away from. That doesn't mean that you can't still make mistakes, or that you shouldn't listen to the people around you; but you do need that instinct to work from. That's where the cumulative experience you gain from years of disciplined, focused work comes into play.

When Eileen and I first started working with Russ von Hoelscher, I'd often come to him with an idea, all excited and eager, and he would just bat it down. He'd say something like, "Nope—sorry, T.J. Forget it, it's not going to work." Sometimes, I got so angry I just wanted to shout at him. I kept my mouth shut, because I respected him; but I wanted to say, "What do you *mean* it won't work? How do you *know*?"

The answer was simple enough: he had over 20 years of cumulative business experience at the time, whereas we were just getting started; we were relative babies in the field. Ironically enough, I now have clients who come to me all the time with ideas, and I want to say the same exact thing to them. Sometimes I do, sometimes I don't. Sometimes I keep my mouth shut, and sometimes I tell them what I think they want to hear. I'll admit it; I'm a people pleaser. **But the thing is, I now know what works (or at least what works best), and what doesn't.** That's one of the payoffs for my decades of putting in all this time, effort, and energy, and thinking about this in the deepest way, and setting the high goals that we then implement with intelligent direction and skillful execution. I just can't think of a bigger benefit.

And there *is* a lot of work required. Back when I was in my early 20s and first got it in my head that I wanted to make millions of dollars, I was poor indeed—so broke I could barely keep a roof over my head. I didn't have a proverbial pot to pee in, but I was ambitious, even though I wasn't blessed with any particular skills or abilities. I was also envious of those who lived in big houses and drove nice cars. I thought they had an edge that I didn't: that they'd gone to the right schools, or that they just had the right contacts. I didn't have any of those things, and I wasn't born rich—and I was so jealous of those people that I would sound off about it to anybody who would listen. Basically, I was a just a big baby feeling sorry for myself. That's about all it was.

One day, one of my good friends finally had enough of listening to me go on and on about it—and she blew up at me. I'll never forget how she got right in my face and yelled, "T.J., go to any of those big houses, knock on the door, and ask the people inside, 'What did it take for you to buy this house?' And they'll tell you they had to work their asses off! **They had to pay a tremendous price to live there!"**

While I know that there are exceptions to what she told me, I can look back at that statement now and say, "You know, she was right a whole lot more than she was wrong," because now *I* live in one of those big houses. If somebody came up to my house and saw my nice car, and knocked on my door and asked me, "How did you get this big house? How did you get that nice car?" **I'd say, "I worked my ass off for it!"**

Consistently earning big money over a period of years *never* happens by accident; it requires determination and commitment to long-term goals. It's easier to do something successful once than to repeat it over and over again long-term. The commitment level is different. You could win the lottery and come into millions of dollars, and certainly people do that on a regular basis; unfortunately for them, many of them end up broke within just a few years. You could stumble upon some kind of a fad item or a short-term profitable situation where you make a bunch of money in a flash, and then within a matter of months or years it's all gone and you're back to where you were before.

Certainly, none of us would pass up those kinds of scenarios. Most of us would be willing to make a million dollars really fast and then hope for the best afterward; I'm sure, for example, that most of us would be happy to keep any lottery winnings. We're not going to say, "Nah, I'm not going to keep that because I didn't earn it over a long period."

But windfalls like that are accidents. It's much harder to build a sustainable success. **Anything can happen any day; but long-term success requires high intention, sincere effort, intelligent direction, and skillful execution.**

Let's look more closely at high intention. It's not just any intention, and certainly not just casual intention. Are you focused on the goal of making big money consistently over a long period of time? Are you focused and committed to doing whatever it takes to be successful? That high intention has to be there. **If there's no intention, then you'll be unfocused, you'll waiver, you'll be uncommitted. And then there's sincere effort. Are you *really* doing what it takes to succeed?** When I read stories

116

about athletes and the dedication they require to succeed at their sports, or the training that an Olympian goes through to compete at that level, I see the sincere effort that they've expended to be the best they can be. Consider an NFL athlete. There are lots of kids who play football in junior high. There are a few less, but still quite a few, who play at the high school level. And then there are the scholarship positions at the colleges, and even those are limited in comparison to the number of people who are playing college football. But that number is still fairly large compared to the number of people who actually make it to the NFL, with their 53-man team rosters.

Think about the NBA, which plays five people at a time; generally, their benches include only a handful of people who aren't actually playing at a given moment. So it's even harder to become an elite NBA player, even though a lot of kids play basketball as kids. **But what separates a kid playing at a sport from a professional in the big leagues—NBA, NFL, MLB, NHL, whatever—is the pro's commitment to long-term success: their sincere effort and high intention.**

It also takes intelligent direction to get where you need to go. **You have to point yourself in the right direction based on the objectives you're trying to reach, then occasionally make slight changes in your course to maximize your success.** You're sort of like a ship or airplane; the pilot or navigator has a set destination in mind from Point A to Point B, and intelligently redirects the vessel when it drifts off course. If you were to plop a boat down in the middle of the ocean without intelligent direction, it would just float at random based on the winds and currents. It would eventually get somewhere, but who knows where? Life, and business life, can be like that if you allow it. But if you're looking to build long-term sustainable success, to make big money consistently over a number of years and maintain a career in business, you have to intelligently point your life in the direction of achieving those goals.

Getting there also requires skillful execution. Now, the idea that you can just do things and that you'll get somewhere is partly right. **It does take action—but to really get where you want to go takes** *skillful* **action.** This is closely allied to intelligent direction; you have to be able to execute things properly to achieve your goals. Recently, Chris Lakey was listening to one of his children talking about practicing for something, and Chris threw out the comment, "Practice makes perfect." But after thinking about that for a while, he realized that the truth was something a bit different that he's heard before: ***"Perfect* practice makes perfect." If you practice wrong all the time, you're going to end up executing wrong;** and if you climb the wrong mountain, you won't end up achieving what you set out to do in the first place. **Skillful execution, not just practice, results in hitting the target. You've got to know exactly what you're practicing for to get it right.**

Mix together all those factors—high intention, sincere effort, intelligent direction, and skillful execution—and you end up with intentional decisions that take you as directly as possible from where you are to where you want to be, rather than just floating through life and hoping for the best. **This formula results in wise, productive choices.** Sometimes, those choices hinge on relatively small decisions, like deciding whether to spend a weekend in Vegas with your friends, or a weekend working on a project that you're trying to get perfect.

Now, you might think, "Well, it's not really that big a deal. I'm going to go out for the weekend. I'm going to enjoy myself and get some R & R. When I come back, the project will still be here waiting on me; but I just really need this time away to refocus." And that's fine; as an isolated event, you may be right, and deciding to go out with your friends may be either helpful in the long run, or at least won't make much difference. But if you string too many of those events together, you can hurt yourself productively. **Sadly, most people have a tendency towards laziness. It's always easier either to do nothing, or to take the path of least resistance.** That's why it's easier to eat ice cream than salad, or sit and watch TV rather than take a bike ride. We tend to gravitate toward the easiest things.

We're all going to look back on today, whether 10, 20, or 30 years in the future. **Those who are the most successful will see that they were consistently intentional about their efforts; they refused to sell themselves short, and refused to take the easiest way out.** They did all they could to achieve maximum output. That attitude sets people apart in the business world, making them the ones that everybody else looks up to. So when you look to your business heroes and say, "Those are the people who have achieved what I'd like to achieve," realize that they got there by doing things differently than most people are willing to do. **If you want to be like them, then you have to be different too.**

If all this sounds like too much work for you, let me just say this: the more you want something, the easier it is to achieve it. Oh, you'll still be working hard, there's no doubt of that; but it won't *feel* like you're working that hard. **So set high goals that you can be excited about, so you're more likely to want to reach the target. The bigger it is, the more it excites you, the more it fires you up, the easier it will seem.** Often it won't even feel like work at all, which is one of life's little ironies.

The author Richard Bach turned me onto that idea. His most famous book is a fast read called *Jonathan Livingston Seagull*. **Bach once said, "The more I want something, the less I call it work." And that was incredibly wise, because that attitude works very well.** If you keep your eyes on the prize, setting your intentions so high you'll be willing to go through hell to achieve them, it won't even *feel* like hell most of the time.

And there's another point I want to make here: the world is filled with late bloomers, folks who didn't start achieving phenomenal success until their later years. One of the reasons they didn't was because they didn't find out what they really wanted to do until late in life. **They had to go through a lot of what they didn't actually want before they discovered what was important to them. But once they did, they caught fire—and nothing could stop them.** They used their accumulated years of experience and wisdom to quickly gain everything they wanted.

So don't be discouraged by any of this. It does take time, it does take work, it does take effort. **But the more you want it, the easier it will be—and the faster it will come to you.**

CHAPTER NINE

"I've seen companies so obsessed with competition that they keep looking in their rearview mirror and crash into a tree."

— *Sergey Brin*
Co-Founder of Google.com

Don't Get Too Obsessed
With the Competition!

Sergey Brin, the co-founder of Google, once said to *Forbes* magazine, **"I've seen companies that are so obsessed with competition that they keep looking in their rearview mirror... and then they crash into a tree."** There are so many great things to say about this quote, not least the fact that Google has made billions of dollars. They're an extremely innovative, aggressive company, out to dominate the Internet; so when this man speaks, we should all listen.

Competition is a complicated thing, and I'm not going to be able to hash it all out over the next few pages. That would take a whole book, at the very least. **But one thing you should know is that all competition is good, and that you should indeed pay close attention to it, because it points the way.** When there are a lot of competitors in a marketplace, that means the market is strong, because obviously it contains a lot of buyers who want the types of products or services sold in that market. **Therefore, you do need to study your competition, because their actions teach you the right things to do—as well as the wrong ones.**

Not only should you strive to identify the best competitors in your market, **you should do business with them anonymously.** Don't use your real name; have somebody else join their mailing list on your behalf. This is a form of "corporate espionage," I suppose; but it's legal, so there's nothing immoral about it. Just get on your competitors' lists, and buy stuff from them. Try to see what's behind their most effective advertising. **Your challenge is to look at their marketing not with the eyes of a customer, but in an objective fashion from the other side of the cash register.** This can help you determine what they're doing right, and what they're doing wrong.

But don't spend *too* much time studying them—and never just copy what they're doing. Needless to say, nobody wants to be a plagiarist; and there are laws against plagiarizing anyway. But the real danger here comes from that fact that you can't usually copyright an idea, so the whole market is filled with people just following the follower. **There's very little innovation, and you need to avoid that at all costs.**

So while you do need to keep an eye on your competitors, be careful about it—and stop looking backward all the time. Rather than fix your eyes on the rearview mirror, keep them on the road. You can't constantly keep your eyes on the competitors. Yes, learn from them, study them, get on their lists, find out what they're doing right and try to break it down so you can emulate it; **but remember, your job is to innovate as well, to make the things you're emulating even better than the originals.** Always strive to develop your own individual products and services, driven by your unique selling position.

Let's look at a good example: Ray Kroc of McDonald's fame. Kroc didn't start the McDonald's restaurant chain, but he built it into the market leader that it is today. Back in the 1960s, when Kroc was really getting in gear, there were a bunch of

124

companies in the fast food market—including quite a few chains that are long since gone. They didn't make it in the marketplace long-term, but at the time, they were hot on Kroc's trail. During that period, a reporter asked Kroc, "What about all these hundreds of competitors that are springing up now? They're just taking over in all these little towns—and they're copying you. How do you feel about that?"

Kroc said, "It doesn't bother me a bit, and here's why: We're going to innovate faster than they can copy."

I love the spirit and energy reflected in that quote. Ray Kroc wasn't worried about the competition; **he was focused on being the best he could possibly be, and on doing things that none of those copycats could possibly do.** He was always changing the McDonald's marketing tactics, always trying to make things better, always looking for ways to improve, always looking for ways to be the *leader.* Followers are a dime a dozen, and chances are, even if they make a little money at first, they're not going to be able to keep it up. **If you don't constantly do things that are new and different, you're not going to last in the marketplace**—and as a life-long salesman, Kroc knew that in his bones.

The market's filled not just with me-too followers, but with people who are outright breaking the law and ripping off advertising copy. They'll steal anything—but in many cases, the biggest companies in the market don't bother to go after them, because they know that those companies aren't going to last. **The only people who really last in any marketplace are the innovators.**

My best friend owns a very successful pest control business that's been around for about 30 years now; she's owned it since 2001. I helped her with her marketing early on, so I got really familiar with the whole "bug business" and spent a lot of time with her general manager. Kerry Thomas has been in the bug business for many years, and he's a walking, talking encyclopedia on the subject. Now, they're located in Wichita, Kansas, which isn't a very big market; there's maybe half a million people in the metropolitan area. And yet when I was working with them, they had over 100 local competitors.

My friend's company is a premium-priced company, and they've got all these competitors selling the same basic services for less money. Of course, many of those were watering down their bug spray and cutting corners, and not delivering the goods... but still, there were over a hundred competitors! And so I asked Kerry, "Doesn't it bother you that there are so many competitors right here in the Wichita area?" And Kerry said, very matter-of-factly, **"Well, we've got over a hundred competitors... but we've got *no* competition."** I just love the bravado behind that statement. It's reflected in their slogan, too. The name of the company is Midwest Pest Control, and their little slogan goes, "If you want the best, call Midwest."

They're striving to be the best, so their eyes aren't focused on the competitors. **Their eyes are on the road ahead.** Midwest is intent on discovering what it takes to serve their customers in the highest possible way, and on how to give those customers more of what they want the most. Kerry and company ask themselves constantly, "How do we keep serving it up bigger and better? How do we own the marketplace? How do we become the competitor that everybody else is scared to death of?" That needs to be your attitude, too. That needs to be your spirit.

Again, I'm not telling you to completely ignore your competition. In his book *Made In America*, the late, great Sam Walton claimed that he had personally been in more K-Mart stores than any other human being on Earth—including K-Mart's executives. K-Mart is (or used to be) one of Wal-Mart's greatest competitors, and they predate Wal-Mart quite a bit. Well, he did a lot of market research in their stores... and he said that he'd gotten thrown out of more K-Marts than anyone in history. After a while it got to be a running gag: someone would say, "Hey, Sam's in aisle #10," and they'd find him there with a little legal pad, writing down their prices and merchandizing strategies.

His kids hated how, whenever the family went on their vacations, Sam had to stop at every single K-Mart store—and every other discount store too. They'd wait in the parking lot while Dad was checking out the competition and learning things from them. **K-Mart and his other competitors helped point the way for him; they'd spot or set trends, and he was just trying to stay ahead of the curve.** Nonetheless, that wasn't his primary focus. **His main goal was giving people a great selection for the lowest possible price, and that's what he strived to do and be the best at.**

That's what you have to do, too. You have to develop your own unique selling position, let other people follow you, innovate faster than they do, and focus on your customers. **Develop solid relationships with them, offering them more of what you know they want the very most.** Give them more of what they bought from you the first time, with a slight twist to make it a little different so that people maintain their interest.

Always ask yourself how to do that—not only for your existing customers, but for all the people in your marketplace who aren't your customers *yet.* **How do you keep giving them more of what you know they want the most, while making it slightly different each time?** That's something of a riddle, though not as self-contradictory as it sounds; but it's something you're never going to have the complete answer to, so you'll have to figure it out as you go. As long as you stay ahead of the game and innovate, you'll come out ahead.

To use a compelling simile, it's like driving on a very dark night. As long as you've got a good vehicle, you're on a good road, you're not driving recklessly, and your headlights illuminate the 50 yards of pavement ahead of you, you're going to be fully safe getting to where you want to go. It's the same thing with running a company: don't overrun your headlights. Practice these ideas, **don't get too freaked out about the competition, keep your eyes on the road in front of you, and look for more ways to serve your customers.** Do that, and you'll own those customers. Maybe they'll continue to do a little business with your competitors, but if you solidify your relationships enough, they'll do most of their business with you.

Speaking of focusing on the road, here's an odd little factoid: Chris Lakey's 1995 BMW, which he just purchased, doesn't have any cup holders (a fact he didn't know until he'd actually bought it). While that seems odd to us Americans, the lack of cup holders wasn't an accident: this car was made to drive really fast on the German autobahn, which has no upper speed limit. When you're zipping along at 100 miles an hour, you have to focus on the road; you don't want to mess with cup holders, because they're dangerous distractions when you're going that fast.

On the autobahn as in business, you need to be focused almost exclusively on what's ahead of you—just like a racecar driver. While you need to be aware of what's around you, seeing every bump and curve ahead is absolutely critical for your safety. **You can move forward extraordinarily fast as long as you stay focused on your mission, and you can respond agilely if you don't worry overly much about what's happening around or behind you.** I'm not a big NASCAR fan, but I've seen some massive flaming pile-ups before. It always amazes me how, while some cars are flipping and tires are rolling all over the place, other cars just zip around it all, somehow navigating through it—even, sometimes, those that are in the middle of the mess as it's happening. That takes a huge willingness to concentrate on exactly what's ahead without being distracted by the action in your peripheral vision. It's difficult to ignore, but you can avoid becoming a victim of the pileup happening around you if you stay task-oriented and focused on the moment.

I think crashing is a good analogy of what can happen in business when you get off task, and the Sergey Brin quote just hammers this point home. Some business people can become so obsessed with what others are doing that they fail to watch where they're going and end up crashing into a metaphorical tree. **Look, you have no control over your competition, except insofar as you can do things that draw people to you instead**

of them. If competitors are crashing and burning on all sides, does it do you any good to try to manage that chaos when you have your own car to steer? Not at all. Even if you glance away for just a second, you can get off the track pretty quickly, and end up running into a wall at 200 miles an hour.

Looking behind you even briefly can be disastrous in racing. Similarly, too great a focus on those behind you or to either side in business can result in significant financial problems, up to and including going into bankruptcy and losing everything you've worked so hard to build. These distractions come in all sorts of shapes and sizes. Perhaps you're too focused on what your competitors are doing, rather than worrying about making your products and services the best they can be. Perhaps you've got regulatory issues to deal with; and this can be a real problem, since we live in a highly regulated society. You have everything from tax laws to OSHA to worry about, and the FTC regulates how you promote your products and services. **While you do have to stay aware of these things, you can't spend too much time worrying about every detail, or you'll get distracted—and that might make you crash and burn.**

Keep your eyes on the road and your car between the lines, and you won't *have* to worry much about what your competitors are doing, or who's trying to take your customers. Emulate Ray Kroc, and keep innovating faster than they can copy. **Stop worrying about keeping on top of everything they do; implement your own ideas, and make *them* follow *you*.** Admittedly, modeling yourself after proven success stories has an important place in business; but if you're not consistently original because you're so busy trying to copy someone else, then you'll never truly succeed.

You can't afford to get too obsessed with the competition. If you're constantly on the defense business-wise, you're only going to be reacting, trying to copy what the other guy's doing so you can counter them. Do that too intensely, and the best you'll end up with is unprofitable "me too" products, because you're just trying to do what everybody else is doing in your marketplace. **Well, if you're a leader—if you take that ball, and run for the goal—then you don't have to worry about what everybody else is doing.** You can set the tone and lead the way, forcing others to react as they try to figure out how to counter you. **When you're in that position, you can focus more on serving your customers and giving them what they want.** That will allow you to maintain the attitude that it takes to be a winner in your marketplace.

Ultimately, this concept (like so many) is about attitude. If your attitude is that of a weaker competitor, if you look at the marketplace and you're too envious of your competitors and wish you could be like them—well, that's a follower mentality. Jettison that and take on a leader mentality; get out there on the vanguard of what's happening in your marketplace. **That way, you don't worry about what everybody else is doing, because you're looking ahead at a wide-open marketplace with lots of room to run.**

When you lead the business pack, you set the policy. You set the way the marketplace is going to respond, and you provide the marketplace with the fresh ideas and the innovations it's looking for, so you don't have to worry about your competition. Sure, you're aware of them and you might pay them a fair amount of attention, just like Sam Walton did with K-Mart as he built Wal-Mart. Yes, visit their stores and get yourself on their marketing lists; buy things from them so you know what they do, how they're operating, and how they're serving their customers. **That alerts you to their weaknesses and strengths, even as you're moving ahead as a leader in the marketplace.** But don't overdo it—or like Sergey Brin says, you may crash into a tree because you've let your attention get diverted from the roadway.

Keep your eyes on the prize, and you can be the leader in your marketplace.

We've had our challenges in the past, trying to apply this principle to our own business. Over the years, we've had people who've stolen our sales copy word for word, and used it for their own ends. They basically stole all the hard work we put into it. But we never went after them, because we knew those people would never last in the market—and they didn't. They came in and made a quick buck, but they never did the kinds of things that cause customers to re-buy from you again and again. That requires some real innovation.

Now, this is a lot of work. I'll be the first to admit it. **And yet, the more you want to be the best in your market, the less work it will seem to be.** You'll work harder, but it won't seem so hard. And that's the real secret here, because many entrepreneurs want to hide that fact from the general public. They're out there performing at a very high level, and they lead you to believe that there's something special about them. **The truth is, the only thing special about those people is their level of desire.** They're highly driven to be the best they can possibly be, and they want to see how high is high for them. They're so committed to succeeding that their output is high and they're very innovative—**but all that hard work doesn't seem like a sacrifice, because they're eager to prove themselves and enjoy the end results of all that hard work.**

It's worthwhile; and in the end, the **rewards more than compensate for the amount of work you commit yourself to.**

CHAPTER TEN

Create as many
"businesses within
your business" as
you possibly can.

Create As Many Businesses Within Your Business As You Possibly Can

The more businesses you can create within your parent business, the more likely you are to profitably succeed. There are many ways to do this—and they don't necessarily have to be distinct, completely different businesses.

Here's the premise behind this idea, and I want you to keep thinking about this, because there's very little I can tell you that's more important: **Your customers will always want to buy more from you than you can offer them.** Your customers are insatiable, and they have various needs and desires that you can't necessarily fill... or, at least, that you aren't filling right now. If you can fill those desires, then you have an excellent chance of making a great deal more money. **So diversify, so you can create multiple income streams by offering not just more products and services, but more types of products and services.**

Now, your individual businesses don't have to be separate companies, but splitting them out is a good way to define the individual categories you're offering your customers and prospects, so you can explore those niches as completely and efficiently as possible. We do this constantly here at M.O.R.E., Inc., but we know we can always improve upon this segment of our business. So we're always looking for ways to get better at it, and you should, too. Here are some of the ways that we do it:

First of all, we put our mailing list up for rent, which can be quite profitable. There are rules our renters have to follow, although we know there's some thievery, where people are taking our names and adding them to their own permanent lists. You'll never get around that; in marketing waters, there are always sharks who are happy to rip away a pound of flesh as you pass. At the beginning, we were torn about renting out our list, and this was one reason. We struggled long and hard with the decision, for weeks. When we did start renting out names, we started cautiously, only renting out the names of people who had made inquiries with us but hadn't purchased; **but ultimately, we ended up renting out our lists of active customers as well, including our very best customers.**

That worked out for us, and many of our mailing list renters have renewed their rentals every quarter for the past 20 years. We get a nice, big monthly check as a result; and once it was so big that my wife and I decided to build the swimming pool we'd been contemplating for a while. Every time I jump into that pool, I ask myself, "What did I have to do to get this swimming pool?" The answer is, "Very little." **We just set up a business within the business, and let our mailing list manager do all the work.**

One way we acquire new products and services to fill our customer needs is to get involved in joint venture deals. At this point in our business, we typically just offer our lists to potential joint venture partners and introduce them to the people on the list, whereupon our partners do all the work to put the project together. Sometimes we help a little; sometimes we do little more than cash the checks. **The very best joint venture deals are the ones where you own the lists, and allow other people access to them.** Admittedly, you have to be very choosy, especially when you contribute your personal endorsement. **Choosing the wrong JV deal can damage your relationship with your customers.** Plus, you can't allow your partners to steal your customers, insofar as that's possible.

However, you usually don't have to worry about that; because while they do want your list, **your potential JV partners** *really* **want your endorsement.** Often, they can get your list through a mailing list broker if that's all they want. **But having your personal endorsement makes them more money, especially when you send an endorsement letter with your joint venture partner's offer.** That usually sends the response through the roof.

On top of list rentals and JV partnerships, we also have a special business, 5-Star Mailing Services, that's owned and operated by three of us: me, Chris Lakey, and my stepson, Chris Burgquist. **We're making lots of extra money on the side by providing specialized marketing services to our customers.** Similarly, Drew Hanson, our Sales Director, has his Ad Services business within the business. **He does lots of advertising for our customers, and it puts a few bucks in his pocket.** Now, we could have chosen to hire an outside company to do this, but we decided to keep it in-house. Drew does a very good job of controlling it, so that in the end it works out better as an in-house business.

In the past, we've also offered coaching programs and lots of other side ventures that allowed us to develop

multiple income streams within our main business.
Sometimes our customers ask us why we do this. Naturally, the
first answer that comes to mind is, "We're trying to make more
money." We don't want to insult anybody's intelligence here, so
we're always pretty blunt about that. We're in business to make
a profit; and we can do that by offering people more stuff. **Not
every product or service is right for everyone, so they need to
be able to pick and choose;** and of course, many of our
customers are insatiable. They just can't get enough. They're
going to go do business with our competitors if we don't serve
them, so they might as well just do business with *us*.

That needs to be your attitude, too. **Strive to offer as many
products in as many categories as possible, so your
customers don't have to do business with your rivals.** You
don't have to form a separate company to do so, although you
definitely can if that's more to your advantage.

Our good friend and printer, Steve Harshbarger, works for
his father-in-law, who actually owns the printing company.
Steve brokers deals on the side, both for us and for other clients.
He asked his father-in-law if he could do that; and his father-in-
law agreed, because he knew there were plenty of printing
services his company just wasn't able to provide, because they
didn't have the right equipment. **Now Steve can help fulfill the
other printing needs of his customer base via his print
brokerage business.** He's making tremendous amounts of
money—in fact, he tells me that on a good year, he makes more
money in that second business than he does in his first.

Chris Lakey and I are involved in a retail business that
we're currently trying to expand and do some new things with.

140

We're trying to sell it through a sort of a franchise model, for example. Being a small retail pet boutique, this is definitely a business within the main business. It has to make a profit, of course; **but part of what we're doing by having additional income streams, and additional businesses within the business, is giving it a tremendous advantage over all the other small retail stores in the area that only have one outlet.** They can only make money with their retail store. We have several ways to make money with this store, so it's likely to be very profitable (assuming these ideas of ours work), whereas most other local retail shops are barely making it, or are forced to close after a couple of years. We're going to keep going strong, because we have other ways of generating revenue.

Accomplishing something like this does require significant innovation on your part. **You've got to re-invent yourself regularly; the companies that last the longest and make the most money are _always_ the ones that do the best job of re-inventing themselves.** They're constantly innovating, constantly looking for ways to change, constantly creating businesses within the main business in order to create and maintain multiple streams of income. They do everything they can to strengthen and solidify their competitive advantages; and you need to do the same. As you innovate and test different kinds of business models and various businesses within the business, you might just stumble across one that ends up making you more money than your original business model did. That's happened plenty of times over the years. So keep trying new and different ideas!

Remember: **the premise that this entire principle is**

based upon is the fact that customers will always be willing to buy more than you can offer them. They're insatiable, and have all kinds of needs and desires beyond what your initial product or service fills. Your job is to fill those needs and desires as best you can, so *you* can get their money, instead of letting any of your competitors get it.

You know, for me—as with many people, I suspect—it's hard to remember what life was like before eBay, and its successful business model of providing easy access to most things people want to buy. The same is true of the Internet in a more general sense. In the olden days (before the early 1990s), retails stores basically sold to the local community, though a few worked through mail order. Even when the option to expand to a global market became available, many small business owners said, "Nah, I don't want to sell on the Internet. I just want to do my thing locally." They had forgotten their responsibility to innovate—if indeed, they had ever learned that principle at all.

And then all of a sudden you started seeing far-thinking business owners stepping up and saying, "You know, we're only reaching this little town of 20,000 or 30,000 people... but if we expand to online ventures, we can enter a marketplace of *millions* of people. All it takes is selling our products via eBay or through a website of some sort, and we can make a lot more money." Many businesses adapted to this reality; and some are still doing it today. It's an ongoing process. **Many businesses are discovering that they don't really need a local presence anymore.** They can do away with brick-and-mortar outlets, and many have. **It's cheaper to maintain an Internet or eBay presence than it is to have a retail storefront—and even**

**beyond that, many stores are making more money on the
Internet than they ever did in a local retail environment.**

These are the people who looked for additional revenue
streams—who looked for businesses within the business—and
ended up succeeding even better with the side business than they
did with the original business. **As a result, their business
model changed radically to reflect that new reality, since it
was simply more profitable than the old way of doing things.**

This can happen to you, too—assuming you're willing to
look beyond what has previously been normal for your
business. Part of this strategy matches what we were talking
about earlier, where if you worry too much about what your
competitors are doing, you can crash and burn because you're
not looking ahead. If you're not a leader, if you just maintain
that old-school mentality and never adapt or adjust, your
business model may die under you. **A big part of being a
successful entrepreneur is always looking for what's next,
always trying to discover the next big thing.** Basically, it all
boils down to grow or die; if you stagnate in place, you may
miss out on a whole new revenue stream that could be more
profitable than what you're already doing.

**Another reason to keep multiple income streams in
place is because you never know what's going to happen in
business; and at the same time, you never know where a hot
idea is going to come from.** One of the things I've talked about
elsewhere is this idea of taking massive action, and putting
yourself in a position where you're throwing a lot of ideas at the
wall to see what sticks. The only way you can do that is to put
yourself in line to do a lot of things. If you're just sitting there in

your little shop and you've never expanded to the Internet, or you've never tried to come up with an alternate revenue stream or additional ways to make money from your customers, then how do you know what else is out there? You can never know what you're missing, and you might miss out on some remarkable way to make more money without doing much beyond what you're already doing.

I've already told you how we financed an entire swimming pool from one month's mailing list rental. All we had to do there was decide to say yes; someone else did almost all the work to bring in the customers, and we got a check. **We're still bringing in substantial income that way, every month. All it took was a decision to create that business within the business.**

If you do decide to sell by mail or on the Internet, *you* should be doing list rental, because it's an easy way to add revenue without adding much in the way of effort. You do have to compile your list and send it to your broker, but they take care of everything else. At the most, you just have to approve who you rent to; and you don't have to be picky if you don't care to be. You can tell your broker to let anyone rent your list without consulting you. Sometimes people do that; sometimes they don't. It's up to you. You'll want to be more choosy with joint venture partners, of course, especially if they ask you to lend your endorsement to their sales; you don't want to get tangled up with someone disreputable. **And of course, you can turn that around.** If you have a hot product or service, you can approach other people whose customers might be interested in that item and either rent their lists, or joint venture with them. **On either side of the equation, you're broadening and strengthening**

your income by adding new revenue streams.

Think of it this way: if you keep all your eggs in one
basket, what happens if the basket crashes to the floor? All your
eggs will crack, and you'll lose everything. Extend this
metaphor further to a nest egg for retirement. If your retirement
portfolio is invested in one specific area, maybe one stock in one
company, what happens if that company goes bankrupt—and
that stock goes from being worth $100 a share to being worth
zero? Simple enough: you lose all your money. Suddenly, your
retirement fund is gone, and you're left wondering what you're
going to do.

Conversely, if you have your retirement nest egg invested
in several dozen different companies, then it probably won't
hurt you much if one does go under. Oh, it's not a good thing,
but it's not going to be too painful because you've diversified.
You have multiple income streams coming into your retirement
portfolio. The same can (and should) be true in your business.
**If you have multiple businesses providing multiple income
sources under one umbrella, you're in a position to weather
the storm when anything happens to you.** If one source of
revenue dries up completely, you're not left wondering what's
going to happen to you.

Let's say that you have a local retail business of some
kind, but you've also established an online presence, where
you're selling to a regional or worldwide marketplace. Well,
suppose your spouse gets a great job in another city, and you'd
really like to go; or your local business experiences hardship for
some reason. Maybe taxes have gone up, and that's hurt your
ability to make a profit; you've had to raise your prices, and

145

customers haven't really liked that. Or let's say that they zone you out; they're going to come in and build a highway right through town, and they're knocking down the building where you've had a store for 20 years. Well, if you're only relying on the revenue from that local store, you'd better hope your new location is as good as your old one, and that your customers will migrate to it. **On the other hand, if you have an Internet-based income stream, it's easier to give up that local presence, for whatever reason.** With a diversified revenue stream, you don't have to worry so much about things going wrong with your primary business.

As another example, let's say you have an information marketing business, where you're selling some kind of information product. **You can add different kinds of revenue streams to that front.** Maybe you've got a newsletter; well, you could create a coaching program to go along with your newsletter. You could write books, or combine your newsletters into books that you could then sell. You could produce audio versions of your writings. You can do all these things and more to supplement your basic information product. **Realize that if customers like to receive one kind of packaged information from you, they're probably going to like it in other formats as well.**

Maybe you can produce live events; for example, you can have one event a year to start with, and later expand it to two, three, or four events per year in order to add new products and services, and therefore new income streams, to your portfolio of business and marketing solutions. **Whatever you choose to do, these things exist to protect you from financial calamity in** one area, while allowing you to pursue new revenue sources and, ideally, entire new categories of business.

You never know when one of those revenue streams is going to turn into the big moneymaker that you've always hoped for. So continue to expand; continue to look for new ways to create revenue sources within your business. That way, you'll not only be more profitable, you'll diversify and protect yourself from failure in any one area.

CHAPTER ELEVEN

Go out of your way to show people that you are <u>REAL</u> and vulnerable — and they will emotionally open up to you.

Show People
That You're For Real

If you go out of your way to show people that you're both real and vulnerable, they'll emotionally open up to you.

I learned this a long time ago, and it's a lesson that's been worth many millions of dollars to us. We were advised right from the beginning, "Never try to be a guru. If you do, first of all you're never going to build long-term bonds with your customers; and second, there's just too much pressure in trying to have all the answers. **It's better to just be perceived as a friend to your customers.**"

Now, here at M.O.R.E., Inc., we love teaching all our wealth-making strategies to people; it's one of our passions! But we've never tried to present ourselves as gurus. We're not perched high up on a mountaintop looking down on everyone. We never pretend like we have all the answers; we don't. Nobody does; anyone who claims otherwise is a big phony. A big part of this strategy is connecting with people, and you can't connect with people if you're too busy being a fake.

Most gurus don't even try to build long-term relationships with their customers. That's one of the reasons that people who are attracted to gurus tend to go from one expert to the next. **It's more effective to position yourself as a friend to your customers and clients;** sure, you're here to teach them all you can, but you're no better than they are. You just know a little more than they do; otherwise, you're still learning.

So don't hesitate to tell stories that humanize you; and if necessary, use a little self-depreciation to make people more comfortable with you. Project yourself as no different from the people you're trying to serve. You've simply learned some things that they need to learn and, if they're willing to learn those things from you, then they can have whatever benefits you've acquired. That's been our positioning strategy for decades, and it's been worth a fortune to us. It can be worth a fortune to you, also.

I see so many marketers these days who are scared to tell their stories—who are scared to be themselves. You read their ads and sales letters, and there's no personality there; there's no mention of who they are or where they come from. **They avoid making any connection with their prospects, and that's a huge mistake**—because everyday people want to do business with other everyday people. **The general marketplace hates phonies.** We prefer to do business with those who have been where we are, people who have figured out a few things on their own, folks we can really connect with.

I understand the instinct to hide. For the first five or ten years of our business, I was afraid to be myself—especially in the seminars and teleseminars we were doing back then. In fact, I was *terrified* of communicating as the real T.J. Rohleder; and so I was always on guard about that. Now, it wasn't that I was being fake or phony; **I was just afraid to fully be myself.** I tried to watch everything I said carefully, because I didn't want to offend anybody; I was so worried about what other people were going to think about me. **It was only when I learned how to let go of all of that that I became a much more powerful communicator,**

and that's certainly taken a lot of pressure off me.

Your clients don't want you to be too professional and polished; and if they do, they aren't the kind of people you want to attract anyway. **It's all about being yourself in ways that people can relate to, with the entire focus being on them and what you're trying to offer them.** Emphasizing their needs over your own is a very powerful tool that will help you get over this paralyzing fear of being yourself, if for no other reason that you don't have time to worry about you when you're putting all you energy into helping them.

Stop worrying about what other people are going to think. When you conduct a large presentation, put all the focus on your prospects and the benefits they're going to receive from you. Put them at ease with some self-depreciating humor. **Tell them some personal stories about yourself—ideally, stories that relate to the benefits you're trying to present.** Never forget that people want to do business with other people they can trust. Understanding and sympathizing with someone is a part of the process of developing such a trust.

The more you try to be polished and perfect, and wall yourself off, the phonier you'll be. Not only will maintaining the façade put you under a lot of pressure, you're going to scare off a lot of people, because they're going to sense that you're holding back. They're going to sense that you're watching your words very carefully. If you're deliberately trying to be some kind of a guru where you act like you've got all the answers, that's even worse. It's one thing to be an authority; it's another to be a know-it-all. If you're not careful, then there's a very good chance that all you're going to do is turn people off.

153

Some of the most powerful communicators I've ever listened to, people who have made the deepest impression on me, have been very real, raw, and human. **They make mistakes, and they don't try to hold back.** In fact, they often tell stories about the mistakes they've made, laughing at themselves a little, and then they get you to laugh at them and some of the dumb things that they did.

Recently, I read a wonderful book called *The Happiness Project,* by Gretchen Rubin. Normally, I shy away from books like this; when I was much younger, I read a lot of self-help books, but the older I get, the more they turn me off. They tend to be too preachy, and I don't like to be preached at. But this book is absolutely incredible, because Ms. Rubin does just what I'm talking about here. She is real, she's raw, she's vulnerable, she tells it like it is. She lays out her own personal story — and she's taken a lot of criticism for that. In her book, in fact, she writes that people often tell her, "You talk about yourself too much."

The truth is, she only talks about herself as it relates to her struggles to learn the kinds of things she's now trying to teach you. **Discussing what she had to go through helps her connect with her readers; it makes things so personal and emotional that it opens people up.** I recently bought five copies of her book so I could give them to a few of my close friends; and I pre-ordered her next book. Plus, I went to her website and signed up with her blog. I'll be a customer for life!

People in your marketplace want to feel that you're honest, open, and real — that you aren't holding anything back, or trying to be phony or superior. In fact, here's a little dirty secret that infests most human souls: Most people *want* to feel superior. Some of us have this problem worse than others; some don't have it at all, and some who do have learned to transcend it. But in general, it's an integral part of human nature.

Well, when you turn it around on people and make it seem you're trying to be superior to *them*, they're offended by that. People resist the idea that you're up there on high, preaching all the received wisdom to them down below—that they should naturally listen to you because you've got it all figured out. **That attitude changes when you start humanizing yourself.** When you talk about your own insecurities and fears, revealing some of your past failures, you become vulnerable. **Now your prospects feel less threatened; and as a result, they become more open and receptive.**

So just be yourself, amplified. This lets you connect with people.

At the same time, of course, you've got to maintain an attitude of salesmanship. You can't just tell a bunch of dumb stories about yourself that have nothing to do with what you're trying to sell. But do go out of your way to show people that you're just like they are. **Be honest with them.** They'll forgive you for not being polished and perfect, as long as you've got the goods and they feel you can deliver on your promises. **Presenting yourself like this will separate you from all those other people who are afraid to do this, and who are *not* doing it.**

Start paying attention to all the people who are sending you marketing materials, ostensibly trying to do business with you, but who are keeping their real selves hidden. Ideally, they want to start a relationship that will lead to you doing business with them over a period of years—even a lifetime—and yet they're doing nothing to build an empathetic relationship with you, to let you know who they are or what they're all about. They especially aren't telling you stories that make them seem like normal human beings. Those are the people you should be doing the opposite of, because it'll put you light years ahead of them.

Why don't other marketers do this? Why do they act like it's some kind of grand secret they're not privy to? **Because most people want to hide their feelings and keep to themselves. That's how we've been taught by society: not to be open and real with other people.** We keep our guards up; we don't like to show our emotions or otherwise put anything out there that might make us look like we don't know what we're doing. And that may be fine in your personal life, or if you're someone's employee; but if you come across that way as a marketer, you're going to lose out. Even if you don't normally handle yourself openly, even if you're typically an intensely private person, you're best served by learning to open up to your customer base. **Let them know that you are, after all, another human being just like them; and that you have some of the same fears and concerns they have.** Maybe you *don't* have it all figured out.

Now, presenting yourself in that way may be scary to you; it may feel like the wrong thing to do. I think we all tend to have this guru mentality in business—that if someone is seeking you out to do business with you, then you have to be the "authority" to their "supplicant." But you don't want them to look at you that way, because that type of relationship can hamper your ability to do business with them. **In trying to be superior to them, you lose that feel of genuineness. You're not one of the**

guys anymore.

This breeds a kind of celebrity mentality among your prospects. Think about how you might feel about meeting your favorite movie star. When you meet that person, yes, you know intellectually that they're just like you. You know that there's nothing special about that person as a human being; **what's special is the relationship,** because you perceive that they're up there on a pedestal somehow, if only because society has placed them there. Well, it feels awkward when you encounter them, doesn't it? Usually the awkwardness goes both ways, sometimes because the celebrity has in fact mentally placed him- or herself in a higher position; but a lot of that sensation comes from you. Putting them up on a pedestal creates a certain tension in the relationship. Maybe you've never even thought about that before, but the tension is real because you're not equal. You see them as an authority, and perhaps they see you as one of the little people.

If you're just hanging out with a buddy over the water cooler, or drinking a beer and watching a movie with them, there's no tension there because there's no threat coming from either side. There's no feeling of imbalanced power or superiority vs. inferiority. You're just two friends hanging out; you're more or less on equal footing. **That results in an open relationship where you can share freely, without any complexities.** It's just what it is.

Now, there's nothing wrong with being a guru, because gurus can be very helpful if you need their help. Certainly, there's some level of earned respect there. For example, I'm no electrician; so if I have a wiring issue in my home and call someone out to fix it, I'd really hope that I can call that person an electrical guru. So that's a perfectly acceptable thing, as long as the prospect or client doesn't get their nose rubbed in the guruship. **Still, inevitably, there's something about that relationship that's different than it would be otherwise if we saw each other as equals.** If I have my buddy come over and fix my electrical system, I'd probably treat him a little differently than I'd treat a pro.

The "guru" idea is just one example of people who carry this banner of being better than you, and of being a know-it-all—whether it's warranted or not. Now, you can have know-it-all friends who are nice; they just happen to be very smart, and when they show this, they're not trying to be rude or act like they're better than you. But sometimes, it feels like they are anyway. You might not even be able to explain that to them, especially when they've given you no real reason to look at them that way; but there's still this tension in the relationship, on both sides of the equation. **They're the know-it-all and you're just you, so the strain is there—even though neither of you intend for it to be that way.** This can be especially damaging if you let it happen in your business relationships.

Consider doctors. I view my doctor as kind of a know-it-all, at least in the health field. This is not necessarily a bad thing; I look to him to be the provider of answers when I have something wrong with me and don't feel like I can figure it out on my own. I trust that I'm going to explain my problem, he's going to examine me, and in the end I'm going to get a solution to the problem. So yes, I see my doctor as a guru in the field of medicine. Now, if it happens that my doctor is a friend of mine, I can chat with him casually about basketball, or joke about him being a Denver Broncos fan and me being a Chiefs fan. If we're buddies, that adds a different complexion to the relationship.

Still, for all that we can laugh and joke as equals, when it comes to medicine he *is* a professional—and I feel like the little dope who knows nothing, even if he doesn't come across to me that way intentionally. **That's just a natural emotional outgrowth of the fact that he's an expert in his field, and I'm not;** but you can't ignore the tension this causes in the relationship. The imbalance there does cause a strain, no matter what.

It can be the same with lawyers. Personally, I know very little about the law, so if I need legal advice, I go to a lawyer and pay them to find the answers for me. Chris Lakey is working with a lawyer right now, as he starts his non-profit organization. He's trying to get tax-exempt status through the IRS, and it's like rocket science. They make it very difficult—on purpose—so Chris is working with a friend who happens to be a lawyer to work it out. He's known her for a long time, and trusts her opinions.

Now, he's never really talked sports with her; but she probably likes some sports, and if they were to talk about those sports, Chris might feel like she was a buddy. But in legal matters, he says, he does feel the imbalance of the relationship; she's the guru, and he's just Chris. The fact that she's an expert in her field creates a different kind of relationship between them. As for the I.R.S. personnel... well, they may not be seen as gurus, but like many other people in the government, they're seen as being "over" you, as if they know more than you do. Whether they do or don't is inconsequential; they wield authority, which makes that relationship different than if you perceived them as equals. That's just the nature of such a relationship.

Don't let your own position of authority hamstring you in business. Use it to your advantage. Open up and show people that you're equals. Let them know you can be buddies, kicking back and talking sports, or just talking shop. Helping your customers and prospects feel that way about you will put them at ease. They'll feel they can trust you in the relationship, and they'll be more inclined to do business with you because of that. Keep this firmly in mind as you develop your relationships with your customers.

This principle really has made us a fortune at M.O.R.E., Inc. We've gone out of our way to tell our story, especially our before and after story, in ways that connect with our clients. As a result, they feel that we identify with them, that we understand them. **And people** *want* **to be understood. They** *need* **to be understood, to know you can sympathize with the pain and the frustrations that cause them to buy the kinds of products and services you sell, which ultimately produce the solutions they're looking for.**

Just be personable with people, and tell them your story. **Reveal the common denominators that connect you to them. Offer the solutions you've found for their pain and frustration while you were trying to ease your own.** If you can do that, they'll not only open up their personalities to you, they'll also open up their wallets. That's the name of the game. In the end, you're looking for customers for life, and this is how to get and keep them.

CHAPTER TWELVE

Love and hate play an important role in the creative process.

❀ To begin a project — you must fall completely and totally in love with it! And while in love — write <u>all</u> of the promotional materials!

❀ And to complete the project — you must <u>hate</u> <u>it</u> in the worst way and want nothing more than to be done with it so you can move on to something else!

Love and Hate Play Important Roles in the Creative Process

To begin a project effectively, and build up the momentum necessary to see it through, you've got to fall completely and totally in love with it. While you're in that emotional state, that's when you come up with many of your greatest ideas, so it's the time when you should develop all your promotional materials. That's when the ideas are flowing like hot lava flows from an active volcano. When that happens, it's the heat of passion that you feel; and it's definitely a form of love.

And then, to complete the project, you've got to come to hate it in the worst possible way. The more you can hate it, the sooner you can wrap it up and move on to something else. During this period, you're better able to identify the best ideas among those you've developed in earlier phases.

Developing a product, service, or campaign is a two-step process, you see; and **one of the biggest mistakes that people make is trying to collapse that process into one step.** That is, they try to come up with ideas, while simultaneously trying to edit themselves. These are things that require two entirely different frames of mind.

In beginning, while you're still in love with your new business idea, don't try to be critical in any way. Part of the secret of effective brainstorming is to throw the filters wide open. No idea is stupid or wrong; you take them all in as equals.

Even if you think it's a bad idea, you bite your tongue. At this stage, quantity and quality are synonymous with each other. **The way to get better ideas is to get more ideas—and you'll do that when you're passionate, when you're excited, when you're enthusiastic.**

Later, when you've exhausted that passion somewhat and come up with as many ideas as you possibly can, **then you have to shift gears and get into that second frame of mind, where you can more objectively identify the ideas that work best.** Now is when you start to attack some of the ideas you came up with in the beginning. **Now you're looking for problems, trying to hone, shape, and polish your concepts to perfect them.** That requires an entirely different mindset: cold, calculated, and somewhat negative (or at least, it could be perceived as such).

Again, a lot of people try to do both at the same time. That's MISTAKE #1. And then there are some people who never shift gears. They're always positive, positive, positive; and that's MISTAKE #2. They never fall out of love with their ideas enough to be able to prepare them for the marketplace. That's a big mistake that we see a lot of wild-eyed dreamers make: they stay deluded. Their ideas are like their babies, and you don't dare say anything bad about them—ever. They never go into that second gear, that second thought process, of falling out of love with an idea and starting to hate it, to the point where they can shape it, fine-tune it, polish it, and get it ready for market.

MISTAKE #3 is attacking the idea when it's brand new—trying to find everything that's wrong from the git-go. People who do this end up killing the baby before it has any time to grow and develop. I think some people do that because that's how their minds work; they're analytical thinkers, so maybe it's easier for them to see all the things that can go wrong than to see all the things that can go *right*. That makes it easier to shoot an idea down in the beginning. And some people just like to feel superior; so every time somebody throws them a new idea, they bat it down as fast as possible instead of taking the time to develop it a little, to see if it might turn into something worthwhile.

Here's a great quote that I memorized years ago, and the older I get, the more I can see the wisdom in it: "If you love something enough, it will reveal all of its secrets." **When you're excited about something** (you don't have to use the words "love" or "passion" if you prefer not to), **then it becomes easier to understand—if only because you're more likely to become thoroughly engrossed in it.**

Sometimes when I write a sales letter, I'll spend a whole day or more just getting everything on paper. Then I'll focus on getting it right—writing and rewriting and going over it again and again, testing new ways of presenting and formatting it. **I might spend 15 hours like that on a short letter of ten pages or less, because I'm completely focused on it—and as I go over it again, I'll see things I didn't see before.** When I do, I wonder, "How did I miss that? It's so obvious! Why couldn't I have said *this*?" The more you love something this way, the more it reveals its secrets to you.

So get passionate about this whole process of falling in love with ideas that you know your customers will love, too—or at least, that you strongly suspect your customers will love.

165

Brainstorm it out in the beginning, coming up with as many different angles as you possibly can. At this stage, no idea is too crazy, so just get it all out there. Have fun with it; stay excited; stay passionate; stay in that creative zone. I'm convinced that there's magic in that creative zone. It's almost spooky to me, how excited I get when I start writing sales copy and all the ideas just start to flow.

Sometimes the ideas come to me faster than I can possibly type them, so I don't worry about typographical errors or punctuation; I can go back and clean all that up later. I don't worry about proper sentences or paragraphs; **I just get it all out.** Sometimes it comes so fast I feel like I'm taking dictation... and I never know quite what I'm going to write, or quite what I've written until I look at it later. That emotional, creative process is just the most amazing feeling.

People who make the mistake of trying to edit themselves as they go are never going to experience that thrill, that joy, that pure passion, that very spiritual sensation you get when you're high on a concept and the ideas are just flowing out of you. **They're never going to come up with as many creative ideas as they could.** This is especially true for the people who try their hardest to kill an idea just after its birth, looking for everything that could possibly go wrong with it before it has a chance to grow and develop even a little.

Rather than kill the baby before it has a chance to grow, let that little seed of an idea bloom. You can cull it later.

I get up very early in the morning, and I start working right away. That's my favorite time of day, and there's a kind of a

magical feel to it. Other people might experience this late at
night; but in either case, it's a quiet time when you can put all
your focus on your task. There's no phone, no fax machine, no
distraction; and all this makes it a wonderful time to dream up
new possibilities and create as many new ideas as you possibly
can. **All this fires your enthusiasm—and enthusiasm sells.
When you're passionate about something, that passion
comes out in your writing.** It comes out in the way you speak,
which brings life to your live presentations and recordings. If
you're excited, people can connect with it—which earns you
more money.

Here's another good point: **Sometimes the less you know
about something, the better you can sell it.** Some people make
the mistake of thinking they have to know every little detail
about a topic, product, or service before they can sell or present
it to someone else. **But sometimes, too much knowledge hurts
you.** Remember: We sell benefits, not features. **Marketing
consists of two type of knowledge: product knowledge, and
prospect knowledge.** The latter means you should know who
you're trying to communicate with, and the benefits you're
trying to deliver; you don't have to get bogged down explaining
all the details. Often people don't even want to know all that,
especially in the beginning. Keep that in mind as you pass from
the love phase into the analytical phase, and become critical of
your idea so that you can shape it into the best thing that it can
be—if, in fact, you decide to continue pursuing it.

**In general, think of this as a two-tiered concept of first
falling in love with your product or service, and thereby
letting it develop somewhat before becoming very critical of**

it, so you can to shape the idea into something useful. As attractive as an idea may be, you can't be like those wild-eyed dreamers who always believe wholeheartedly in their products, refusing to look at anything critically. People like that end up hurting themselves and everybody around them. It takes both mindsets to succeed.

You know, I just love the creative process; it's one of the things I live for. And yet, I like to keep a couple of projects on my plate at all times that I kind of hate. I know I've got to do some work on them... and I don't want to. I've lost my passion for them. **But those projects are very important to me because, as I push through all the things I've got to do, I often come up with my most creative ideas—if only because I'm trying to avoid dealing with those projects.**

Years ago, I was a member of this group of about 20 people who got together four times a year. As part of that, we had to sit around listening to presentations from all the others in the group—and some of them were so boring to me. I can't sit still anyway, and it drove me crazy. But I was required to be there; I couldn't just leave the room every time I got bored. So I pretended I was taking notes while other people were speaking—when what I was really doing was using the pain of the boredom to come up with some really cool, creative ideas. While it looked like I was excited and passionate about everything my colleagues were saying, that smile on my face had nothing to do with them. **This was a case where hating something helped me achieve more.**

I think the love-hate dichotomy I've expressed here is a good model for the way you flow from the early creative stage

168

on through the end of a project. At the beginning you love it to death; by the end you're more than ready to cut the cord. In between, you let the idea mature enough that it can hopefully handle a little shaping—and at some point, your enthusiasm for it starts to wane. **You're in a mid-level energy state. You're still pursuing it, you're trying to complete it, but you don't love it so much—and now you can see its potential flaws.** That's when you *should* see them—not so early in the process that you may toss out the baby with the bathwater.

And then, at some point down the road, that project becomes a thorn in your side. You've had enough; you might even start detesting it because it's not finished yet. Maybe you feel like a student who's up at midnight before a big paper is due, trying to pound it out; and you hate that moment right before you finally have the satisfaction of knowing it's all done. **The pressure is painful as the deadline approaches... and you just abhor everything about it.** But you keep going; you get it finished and you present it to the world, so they can benefit from what you're offering, and you can benefit from the knowledge that the task is now completed.

So both love and hate play important roles in this process of conceiving, developing, and producing a new product concept. At the very beginning you're enamored with it; it's a baby idea. By the end it's like an albatross around your neck, so you hate it. There's no way to circumvent the process, really, even through you know it's going to happen. **You've got to let that idea be born, then develop and blossom to a certain level of maturity, without hindering it.** Don't stamp it out too early; you can't know whether it'll turn into a thistle or a rose. And don't let other people stamp on it, either. Sometimes when you share an idea with somebody, the first thing they do is criticize it. Well, it's easy to find people who will tell you why a certain idea won't work or why this thing you're so proud of isn't feasible or won't function. Some of them might know what they're talking about; those you might listen to, if the argument is sound. Ignore everyone else, especially those inexperienced in your field.

Lots of people will happily give you all of the reasons why you should just quit right now. They'll tell you not to dream, not to put any effort into this project, not to spend any more time on it, not to spend any more money on it... to just stop while you're ahead. Some of them might even be trying to help you when they tell you all this, but it's still bad advice. **So during this beginning phase, while you're in love with your project, don't tell them about your baby idea; guard it with your life.** Put as much energy and passion in it as you can to get past that initial phase, to the point where you're far enough into the project that you can't easily back out.

It's easy to quit a project when the idea's still tiny, because you have very little invested in it. As a result, it dies a quick, painless death. **An untold number of ideas have never gotten off the ground as a result—not because they aren't necessarily good or viable, but because they were deliberately killed too early in the process.**

So when you're in the beginning of a new project and you're excited about it, avoid the temptation to share it with too many people. If you must tell anyone, limit exposure to your closest friends and advisors: people you know will be supportive, or who at least won't try to talk you out of it. **Keep the idea to yourself, and develop it as much as you productively can in those moments when you're excited and passionate about the idea.** Eventually, you'll move past that initial stage when it's easy to kill to a more committed stage, when you've got enough money and time invested in it that you can't just back out now.

From that point on, you'll push yourself forward to completion. At some point after that, you'll get to a place where you're no longer in love with it. The project is long in the tooth, and you just want to see it done. In that moment, a switch will flip and you'll just wish it didn't exist anymore; you'll do anything to get it done, and start asking yourself serious questions about how to get it off your plate. **Moving it forward to a state of completion will become a major goal.**

Maybe all along you've been working on an idea, and you've been tweaking it a bit here, a bit there, with breathers in between. There's been no deadline, nothing forcing you to get it done... so you haven't. It's like an artist who dabbles, never satisfied, or a writer who's never really done with their writing. But give them a deadline, and they can finalize things. **That's what happens when you suddenly get tired of a project; if you've put too much into it to just abandon it, then you've got to set yourself a deadline to finish.** Sometimes, the only way to get beyond the dabbling phase is to start hating it enough to want it to be finished forever. This makes you change the way you think about it. You ask different questions, and start trying to find solutions that get it done faster.

Now, maybe that means you just accept the fact that it's not

171

going to get any better. Or maybe you're trying to invent something, and you've finally got it more-or-less right. You feel like you could possibly do more, but you're ready to call it quits—so you'll save any improvements for the second version, on down the road. **You just need to call it done, so you're going to do whatever it takes to finish it up. The ideas start flowing in a different way, and you stop tinkering with it; now you're serious about achieving your goals.** Otherwise, you'll just be prone to putting more and more time into it. Only by finally flipping the switch will you find the solutions required to get it done.

Love and hate. You've got to have both emotions in play at different parts of the creative process in order to be successful and to move projects along. If you just stay in love with them, you'll keep wanting to play with them. Most artists are like that, whether you're a painter, a musician, or a copywriter; it's hard just to let things be, because your creations are your children, and you do love them. **It's not until you can control that love, and turn it into a species of hate, that you can really finish it up.**

So don't be one of those wild-eyed dreamers who tinkers with their creations forever, and never makes any money off them because they never let them go. **The truth is, you can't see all the things that might be wrong with something until you learn to hate it; then you can really shape it up.** And realize that there's *always* something wrong with your creations, at some level. But don't let this tendency overwhelm you, either. **Don't fall into the trap of killing your ideas before they have a chance to grow and develop into worthwhile concepts.**